THE COMPLETE GUIDE TO
Truck Modelling
VOLUME 2

In memoriam

This book is dedicated to Jan Mostek, a great Czech modeller and a member of the Czechoslovakian and later Czech IMPS.

Jan has dedicated a large part of his life, time and energy to modelling. Although his profession was airlines and aircraft, in modelling he was enthralled by old trucks, and didn't just build models for himself. He contributed to the expansion of plastic modelling as a hobby in general as an author of many articles, publications and the IPMS marking rules for vehicle models in competitions. We first met in 2004 and since then Jan has helped me on numerous occasions, discussing my thoughts, providing me with reference material or drawing decals for my models.

About ten years ago Jan was left partially paralysed after a stroke. He could not build models anymore but he did not get embittered. When he could not build the models himself, he came coming up with builds for other people around him, providing reference, creating drawings and drawing decals for them. Mainly Jirí Hübner could tell as he virtually became Jan's hands. Jan was still attending both the Jabbeke and Gaydon shows with us although it has become far from comfortable for him. It was thanks to Jan's drawings that fantastic resin kits were created (including both the GMC and Pete 350 in this book) and he also made a large amount of decals for me: Joseph A. Mrazek on the GMC, the PIE on Peterbilt or Audo Viktoria on the Iveco in the previous book.

Jan died on 31st November 2016. Let this book belong to him as the man who helped to clear the paths we are walking today in comfort. He should never be forgotten.

From left to right: Jiri Hübner, Karel Krejci, Jan Sklenicka, Ladislav Petrik, the author and Jan Mostek in Gaydon, 2013.

The Complete Guide to Truck Modelling vol.2
©Canfora Publishing 2020
ISBN 978-91-984775-7-3
Project manager: Toni Canfora
Design: Toni Canfora
Print: Finidr s.r.o, Czech Republic

Canfora Publishing / Grafisk Form&Förlag
Upplandsgatan 96A
113 44 Stockholm, Sweden
info@canfora.se
www.canfora.se

CONTENTS

CHAPTER	PAGE
01. PAINTING AND DECALLING	4
02. WORKING WITH PHOTO ETCH	20
03. BUILDING A FRAME FROM SCRATCH	28
04. WEATHERING - A REFERENCE GALLERY	34
05. CAB INTERIORS	50
06. TRAILER KITS AND TRAILER REFERENCES	60
07. SCHMITZ CURTAINSIDE TRAILER	72
08. PETERBILT 350 WITH FRUEHAUF DRY VAN	84
09. AMERICAN TRUCK FEATURES	100
10. PETERBILT 359	108
11. GMC CANNONBALL	120
12. VOLVO F12	132
13. FERGUSON TE-20 "FERGIE"	144
14. MERCEDES 1222 LF16 FIRETRUCK	154
15. GALLERY	164

1 PAINTING & DECALLING

There are a several topics I have often found myself discussing with other modellers in recent years, no matter how experienced they are. Some may seem rather basic and essential when finishing a model, but many constructors of scale models are still uncertain of how to address these topics.

therefore decided to dedicate a few separate chapters to describe these subjects, providing a robust foundation on which everyone can rely. The main areas are paints and painting models in general, working with photo-etched metal parts and adding colour to natural metal surfaces using different metallics. On top of this, there are various tech-tips highlighted throughout the book.

1.1 PAINTS AND PAINTING

I usually do not describe my painting in detail, and nor do I discuss the paints I use because in general there is nothing special about what I do. However, some builders of truck kits still struggle with paints and painting. Yes, all the information is available in many forms, but it can often be confusing, and the reliability questionable – especially on the internet. Let's discuss painting the models in a few short sections to find out how good paints should work, differences between paint types, and what is important for achieving a smooth surface.

1.1.1 SURFACE QUALITY

A clean working environment is vital for any painting. If a clean and smooth paint job is desired, always wash the parts beforehand. An old brush and warm soapy water will suf-

For me there is just one primer that meets all the requirements and that is the Mr.Primer Surfacer and its variations.

fice. This will remove any dust and dirt from the model's surface but also washes away any grease that tends to capture debris and dust. Some paints are very sensitive to a grease on the surface (especially the acrylic water-based variety); some paints cope with this a lot better but washing the parts prior to spraying is recommended in any case. I always wipe out any dust from the painted part right before spraying with a Tamiya anti-static brush, which significantly reduces the amount of dust trapped on a surface.

1.1.2 PRIMERS AND PRIMING

When spray-painting models, using a primer is always recommended. It helps with paint adhesion and unifies the model surface, avoiding any colour or structural variation, especially when the model consists of parts made from different materials (plastic in different colours but also resin, brass or even wood). Additionally, primer helps to reveal any surface issues such as scratches or places where putty was applied but not sanded properly.

There are certain properties all good primers should have. It should work as a super-fine body filler that helps to remove fine surface scratches and imperfections. It should have a neutral colour (so you can apply any shade over it) and it's desirable for it to dry quickly and be easy to sand – so adding more paint layers and sanding can be done speedily. For me there is just one primer that meets all the requirements and that is Gunze Mr. Surfacer and its variations. It is available in different grades colours. The basic range comes in a relatively neutral grey (and can be mixed with Mr.Color if needed) but also as Mr.Finishing Surfacer Black, Mr.Mahogany Surfacer (brown) and Mr.Oxide Surfacer (red brown).

1.1.3 PAINTS

I do not like writing about paint brands in general because in different parts of the world you normally get different paints and thinners,

and one of the most important features is retail accessibility. Having a nearby shop where you can get your paint quickly is priceless, especially when you are in a middle of a project and run out of something. However, I see many people around me struggling with choosing the right products and there is a basic level of information about paints that everyone should now. I am not a chemist, so the way I see and describe the reality may seem oversimplified, for which I apologise. There are three basic paint types: traditional enamels, more environmentally friendly water-based acrylics and smelly lacquer paints.

The enamels are probably the first type

Mr.Surfacer from Gunze has been my standard primer ever since I discovered it.

The primers come in spray cans too. It saves time and is also very efficient on larger parts such as cab shells or trailer bodies.

most of us discover. Mostly made by Humbrol, Revell and Testors, enamels were the most common from around 30 years ago. They are fine to spray with an airbrush but can be applied by brush as well. They need a dedicated thinner and have a distinctive odour, which means spraying them in your living room is somewhat problematic. They come in both gloss and matt variants and achieving a high-gloss surface with them is not a problem. They dry in hours or days depending on the layer thickness, and they may not withstand the use of oil paints, which are commonly employed in many modern weathering techniques. But they have some advantages and can still be used for modelling, although in general they have been surpassed by acrylics and lacquer paints due their more suitable properties and shorter drying times.

Acrylics have become more abundant in the last two decades. Made by Tamiya, Val-lejo, Italeri (re-badged Vallejo), Lifecolor and other companies, they can often be thinned just with water and mostly do not smell at all, so they are more suitable for trouble-free indoor use. Some companies provide dedicated thinners to improve their spraying and brushing properties. A retarding agent is usually available, which has a positive impact on brush painting. Acrylics dry virtually in minutes (depending on the layer thickness) and this hastens the painting process considerably. However, the quick drying and general properties mean achieving a high-gloss surface is more difficult in comparison to enamels. Some manufacturers recommend using their retarder (or other additives) for better spraying.

Lacquer-based paints sit somewhere between the aforementioned groups. They have a very strong and distinctive odour and cannot be thinned with water, only with dedicated thinners. Although they are one component their composition and properties are like automotive paints. These have great spraying properties, ensure a hard and glossy surface ideal for fine sanding and polishing, but their brushing performance is rather poor. The most common producer of lacquer-based paints for modellers is Gunze Sangyo with its Mr.Color range, and the well-known Alclad metallic paint range. Tamiya also produces a lacquer thinner which is suitable for diluting its own acrylics (although they can also be thinned with water or Tamiya's own acrylic thinner), which pushes the Tamiya acrylic paint properties towards the lacquer-based too.

1.1.4 SPRAYING AND THINNING

Thinning paint is not a science, but you need some experience to get it right. A well-prepared paint is as important as the quality of the airbrush you use. It is similar to the importance of light when taking photos of your models. You can have a great camera, but if the light conditions are poor the image will never be good enough. It is hard to say that you should use about 50% thinner and the same of paint, as it changes with every paint brand or type. Some paints may need up to 70% thinner when used directly from the original package, and some come pre-thinned for airbrushing. So, what matters is not how much thinner you add to paint but how the latter performs during spraying. I typically start with a roughly 50:50 mixture of paint and thinner, put a few drops into my airbrush and see how it sprays on a piece of white plastic sheet. What drives any additional paint mixing (adding more paint or thinner to the mixture) is how well the paint covers the original surface (it has to be

1. The traditional enamels have been used by modellers for decades.

2. Tamiya acrylics are somewhere between the water based or lacquer based acrylics depending the type of thinner you use.

3. Vallejo acrylics have become the standard brush paint for many modellers and they are ideal for small chips and other detail work.

4. Careful shading of the cab using highly thinned paints, low air pressure and Leveling thinner for diluting the paints. Mr.Color paints are the best ones for this technique.

1. Spray cans may seem a logical way to go when spraying larger parts or when searching for a more specific colour tone. The acrylic ones can be thinned with Mr.Color thinner and blended with Mr.Color paints if needed.

2. Mr.Color paints by Gunze together with Tamiya acrylics, in my opinion the most user-friendly and effective system of paints, thinners and lacquers available on the market, and very suitable for painting car and truck models.

opaque enough) and how the sprayed area edge looks. Well-thinned paint should have a soft transition without any visible droplets or splatters. If there are any droplets and the paint edge is not smooth enough, I add thinner (because the paint is too thick). If the edge is smooth (so there actually is no edge at all), I check how opaque the paint layer is and if necessary, I add more paint and find a good balance between opacity and smoothness. In general, any rough finish (such as the so-called orange peel) actually means the paint was not thin enough or that there was some 'dusting' during spraying, which can also occur, especially with quick-drying acrylics. This is the reason why paint retarders are added for

spraying. It also helps the paint surface to level, stretch and improve the final surface during prolonged drying. There always has to be a compromise: you want the paint to dry quickly so you can touch the sprayed parts and continue building within hours, rather than days, after painting – but you also want the paint to not dry too quickly, because if the paint has time to settle, the quality of finish usually improves.

As for spraying itself, I just want to mention some basics. An airbrush lets you control the amount of paint delivered precisely, unlike aerosol cans. The air pressure for spraying is generally somewhere between 1 and 2 bar (approximately 15-30 psi). The best press-

ure relates to the particular paint density, so it varies slightly; most compressors have an outlet pressure regulator, which allows you to set the pressure correctly. Again, the pressure value should be driven by the way the paint performs during spraying. No visible droplets or splatters should be observed, and these would mean either the paint is too thick, or the pressure too low… or both. On the other hand, when the amount of paint during spraying is hard to control and it immediately collects on the surface (and creates pools), the

3. Working with an airbrush is a delicate job. When thinned properly it allows you to distribute the paint on the model gently with a precise control of the paint quality.

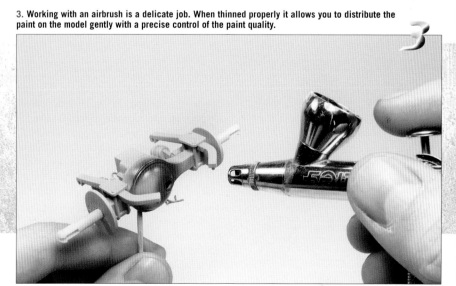

4. The difference between spraying the well thinned paint (below) and a thick paint above is evident. Note the visible individual droplets of the thick paint.

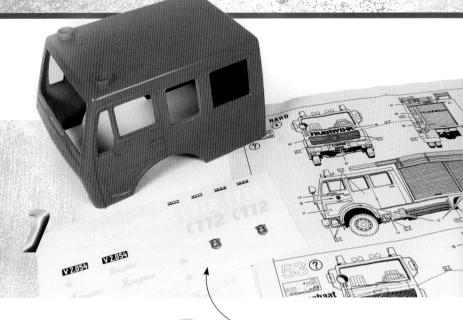

pressure is too high, or the paint too thin. This needs much practice on scrap plastic or old models. Practising on a piece of paper does not help much as the surface properties are too dissimilar to plastic and the paint behaves very differently on it.

1.1.5 DECALS AND CLEAR COATS

A decal is a clear film applied to decal paper on which the graphics is printed. After the decal is placed in a water, the film is released from the paper and may be applied to a model. There are different decals made by various companies and the quality may vary; some decals are obviously more user friendly and some less, but they all work on the same principle. What a decal needs for correct application is a smooth, gloss surface underneath. With a flat and rough surface, you always risk what is called decal 'silvering'. This is when the clear decal film does not adhere to the basic surface fully, allowing trapped air to render the clear film almost opaque. Silvering is a major problem, but it can be remedied by special decal setters and softeners. Setting solution helps adhesion in general and is applied under the decal (I use it for all decals), while softeners do exactly that, helping the decal to suck itself onto raised/engraved surface detail. I use those made by Gunze Sangyo – Mr.Mark Setter and Mr.Mark Softer — but there are different products available.

Even when applied correctly on a gloss surface, the decal film is visible when you take a closer look. I am a perfectionist regarding this, and I really like to have the clear film completely hidden by varnishing. This means that clear coat layers must be applied over the decals and, once the layer is thick enough, it takes just fine sanding before the film and its edges disappear. Decal thickness may differ and so too the number of layers required when using different varnishes to seal the decal perfectly. I have also seen some bad reactions of decals to varnish, so always test

1. Application of decals requires patience and time. Make sure you fully understand the instructions about their placement as you usually have just one try and it has to be perfect.

2. Mr.Mark Setter and Softer are elementary agents used for decal application, but there are alternative products available from other manufacturers.

on a 'dummy' and be easy on the airbrush trigger when spraying the first few coats over the decal.

1.1.6 SANDING AND POLISHING

Sanding is a finishing operation used on the surface prior to painting. Before applying primer, the surface should be already well pre-

pared: fine and smooth. You can always repeat all the sanding and priming after the primer has been applied but working patiently from the beginning, and having the surface good enough, even before priming, saves time. Sanding and polishing in terms of improving the paint finish after its application are regular parts of the process too. Sometimes you get dust in the paint here or there, or the result could be smoother and shinier. Even during sealing the decals, minor sanding may be necessary to help and make the decal clear film invisible.

The appropriate grade of abrasive paper for modelling is somewhere between 400 and 2000. The finer the paper the better. I mostly use those intended for wet sanding as they provide very fine results. When followed by a polishing compound, the 2000-grade paper can even employed, for repairing scratched windows or polishing paints and varnishes. A useful alternative to sanding paper is various sanding and polishing sticks available for model builders. I like to use them all, both rough and fine.

Once the sanding is done, polishing may take place. Although there are different compounds available for wider world purposes, I always stick with the modelling companies. The most popular products are Tamiya polishing compounds (of which the red and blue are most important) and Gunze also provides

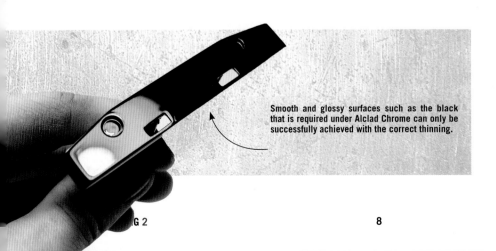

Smooth and glossy surfaces such as the black that is required under Alclad Chrome can only be successfully achieved with the correct thinning.

1. First, the decal is cut from the sheet and placed in water for a minute. Warm water is better than cold, particularly for older decals.

2. Once in place, the excess water and setter is removed. Cotton buds are great for that and I usually roll them over the decal to press it into the surface.

a pair of extra fine compounds ideal for final polishing. As with sanding you always start with the coarse compound and move to finer offerings, step by step, as the surface becomes finer and finer. Dedicated polishing cloth is also available from these two manufacturers and work better than any alternatives. After polishing, the surface may be greasy with compound deposits, which could reduce adhesion of the next paint layer. Therefore, I recommend just fine sanding between different paint layers and let polishing be your very last operation.

3. Humbrol varnishes were my favourites for many years, both for sealing the decals and for coating the entire model.

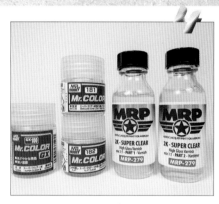

4. Mr.Color lacquers, both gloss and clear, are my first choice for general clear coating. Two component varnishes such as the one from Mr.Paint are the best for high quality car finishes.

Don't get yourself confused. The original GMC paint job was not a 2K varnish. It was actually sprayed with many layers of Tamiya acrylic varnish and polished to perfection with Tamiya polishing compounds.

5. Polishing the painted surface with polishing compounds is very effective. I like to use the Tamiya products for both the compounds and the polishing cloth.

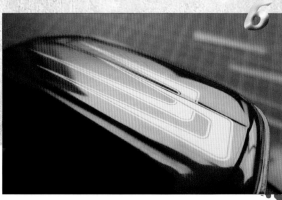

6. Sprayed red, then sanded, decal applied and sealed with 2K clear coat. Then sanded again and polished to a high shine. A typical process to achieve a high quality, glossy surface.

metallics

1.2 PAINTING METALLIC

1.2.1 INTRODUCTION

If there's something that most modellers of classic US trucks consider challenging, it is the number of chrome, polished aluminium and stainless steel parts that must be painted. Aluminium wheels and fuel tanks, chrome bumpers and stainless steel accessories, all are typically found on these vehicles. So let's take a look at some ways to properly recreate these complex finishes.

The kits typically come with pre-chromed parts, but the quality is usually poor. Ejector pin and sink marks, remnants of the technological aspects of the injection moulding process, necessitate the need for clean-up, which of course damages the pre-painted chrome. Often, it's easier for modellers to strip the original chrome finish, repair the ejector pin and sink marks, then repaint the parts with some dedicated metal paint products such as the Alclad II chrome. Another option is to replace the plastic parts with actual metal, such as aluminium on exhaust pipes, fuel tanks, rims and etched parts. When polished, real aluminium looks truly authentic and is easy to touch and manipulate during the model construction process. On the other hand, manipulating parts painted with a metallic paint, such as Alclad, can be tricky.

Knowing what metal is used on different components is essential, especially when building and painting weathered vehicles where the weathering and aging of the metal is different depending on the kind of metal. Chrome and stainless steel weather very differently on real vehicles compared to aluminium. Both

In some kits the chromed parts are brilliant and many can be used directly, while in others, most of the chrome parts need painting.

chrome and stainless steel are relatively maintenance free while aluminium tends to oxidize and take on a very flat, or matte finish. If not cleaned and polished the aluminium surface becomes covered with spots and blemishes. This can be seen in vehicles with aluminium rims and fuel tanks.

Chrome and stainless steel is typically found on bumpers, mudguards and other structural parts such as mounts, supports, mirrors, exhausts, air horns or marker lights. Aluminium is usually used in the making of wheels, fuel tanks and for most catwalks and battery box covers.

1.2.2 REAL METAL PARTS

It may not sound logical to a start chapter on the painting of metal surfaces with a model using real metal parts. However using real metal parts is a quick and efficient way to avoid the complications of painting a metal finish. Metal replacement parts are easily obtainable from online stores, and they look authentic. Use of metal replacement parts on plastic models is becoming quite common place. Most photo-etched products available today, come nickel plated or, in some instances, pre-painted. They are extraordinarily handy for simulating things such as signs, badges and data plates. Photo-etch can also be used to simulate larger parts such as exhaust heat shields and catwalks. Occasionally, you may find larger components, such as rims and fuel

Milled aluminium rims are the typical items that can save time compared to painting the standard kit plastic parts.

tanks, made from machined aluminium. These really look the part and can be polished to a high shine. White metal aftermarket parts are also a common accessory used in building plastic models, though they are not typically intended to be left in their natural metal state.

1.2.3 BARE METAL FOIL

Another great product available to plastic modellers is bare metal foil. Thin, with a self-adhesive on the back, bare metal foil can be applied over nearly any surface. The surface can then be pressed down into all the small nooks and crannies of the model using a burnishing tool, covering all the surface details perfectly with a smooth and realistic result. It can then be polished to a high shine. Bare Metal foil comes in multiple colours, but the chrome and aluminium finishes are particularly handy. I have seen this used on various hood ornaments and on chromed window trims. I've used it successfully on various door or toolbox handles as well as for the reflective surface in mirrors.

1.2.4 PAINTING METAL FINISHES

The reason why I encourage the use of real metal parts, if possible, is that in general, using paint to create a natural metal surfaces is far more difficult than using "normal paint". Painting with normal paints requires precision, but the surface can always be sanded and polished afterwards, so there are options for repair if mistakes are made. However, when using paint to create a metal surface, correcting surface defects after the fact can extremely difficult, if not impossible. The surface must be carefully prepared before applying paint. Therefore, it is essential

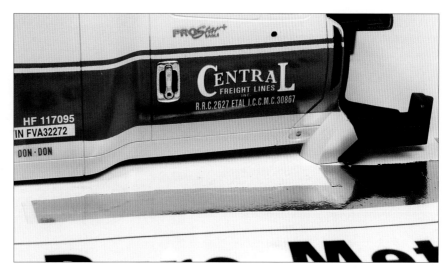

The Bare Metal Foil is a very useful material for making metallic surfaces on various surface details. I have used it succesfully on door handles for example.

Using the BMF foils is also a quick and effective way of making light backgrounds that would otherwise require a difficult painting process.

when painting metal finishes, to take extra care when inspecting the surface quality of the piece being painted. Attention to every minute detail of the surface is necessary in order to obtain a clean, blemish free finish. Failure to take the extra time for preparation will promptly reveal, after applying paint, all the errors you have made or failed to correct in the previous steps. Surface scratches, finger prints, orange peel effect in your primer, dust and dirt collected on the surface will be clearly seen in the final result. The larger the part the higher the difficulty. The higher the part count, the more trouble you can get into. So, if there is a chance to reduce the number of parts you need to paint by using some real metal replacements, it's a simple way to make your life easier. As mentioned previously, it is relatively easy to do this for parts like photo etched data plates, exhaust heatshields, cab or fuel tank steps or catwalks etc. However, there will always be parts on which painting metal finishes can hardly be avoided, and unfortunately these are the usually the largest parts, such as bumpers, radiator grilles, fuel tanks and wheels. There is also the finely detailed accessories that must be painted as well, such as air horns, bullet lights, mirrors and so on.

Another risk factor associated with working with painted chrome and metal surfaces is that they are very sensitive to touch and manipulation. The more you handle them, the more likely you are to damage the surface, even if you use clean hands, gloves or a piece

Alclad Chrome and the dedicated Gloss Black primer, Mr.Paint Chrome, Spaz Stix and the Molotow liquid chrome, are the most common chrome paints of today. Each of them have pros and cons and none of them is perfect.

of cloth to hold the part. Fitting a grille to a hood, or adding PE mesh, lights and logos involves so much manipulation that it is essential to plan and prepare the assembly as much as possible prior to painting in order to make the process as straightforward as possible. Any aids, such as alignment pins or pre-painted assemblies, will likely save you time and prevent you from having to repaint a chromed part damaged with fingerprints.

Since my first attempts at painting chrome back in 2002, I have been using the product Alclad II Chrome. It is my go to product as nothing else has worked as well or has been as easy to use. As the time has gone by, new paint brands and chromed paints have appeared on the market, often describing their properties as better than Alclad or less demanding on the finishing process. I've been skeptical, but I recently decided to try out some of the most common ones on one of my models to make sure I'm not missing anything. So Let's take a moment to compare the available brands and their qualities.

1.2.5 ALCLAD II CHROME

If you're trying to obtain a realistic chrome surface, the brand recommended worldwide is the Alclad II Chrome. This is the first paint I worked with that provided an authentic shiny chrome finish, and I have been using it ever since. Over the years some other off-brand paints have appeared that have limited availability, but the Alclad stands out as the most easily obtainable brand. Alclad also offers a wide range of other metallic paints, from aluminium to jet exhaust burnt metal and more. It comes in glass bottles, pre-thinned for direct application with an airbrush.

In order to successfully apply Alclad you will need some painting skills. Before application of the metallic colour of choice, a base layer of a high-quality gloss black coat is required. Alclad does offer an original gloss black primer in their product line, but virtually any black paint that achieves a high glossy surface will work. The smoother the black layer, the finer the structure of the final chrome surface. If your surface is not glossy enough you will end up with a pretty standard silver finish after your application of Alclad.

Once dry, Alclad II Chrome can be polished, but you must be extraordinarily careful to avoid damaging the surface. I only use very fine tissue paper or cotton ear buds. Alclad will not cover or hide any imperfections, so the black coat has to be really superb. This is where most people encounter problems with the use of Alclad II Chrome. The paint is very sensitive to handling. Once the part is pain-

1. A unique thing about Alclad paints is that they come in a wide array of metallic nuances from which only some are shown in this picture.

2. Mr.Paint vs. Spaz Stix. From the chrome surface quality you can hardly tell the difference. Both are great but don't offer much more than the traditional Alclad Chrome.

ted, any touch may leave some finger prints or blemishes on the surface. Your hands have to be perfectly clean and dry when handling the part, or you should use some kind of fine tissue paper to protect the surface while handling the part.

1.2.6 SPAZ STIX

The Spaz Stix is available in the US and was recommended to me as an alternative to Alclad. Some people have claimed that It was better than Alclad, so I thought I should give it a try. Well, the result is that there is virtually no difference in the finish you get when using Alclad or Spaz Stix. Spaz Stix also requires a super glossy black undercoat. It may be a bit more durable during polishing and manipulation than Alclad, but during the assembly of

my Peterbilt I ended up with fingerprints on the surface that I was not able to remove, so it was necessary to re-paint the whole part. Spaz Stix comes in a plastic bottle and is also pre-thinned for spraying. It's a good product but, like Alclad, it will be unforgiving if you don't pay attention to surface quality and cleanliness before painting.

1.2.7 MR. PAINT CHROME

Mr. Paint is a relatively new range of paints, with properties very similar to Mr. Color paints. Their spraying quality is great, but the odour is very strong. I used them on my Peterbilt 359, and I really enjoyed the experience. They also come in a wide variety of colours, which is always a plus.

As for their chrome paint , it appears to

Molotow Liquid Chrome is not a miracle for spraying large parts. Its strenght lies in the application on smaller parts when brush painting details.

be very similar in performance to Alclad II Chrome and Spaz Stix. As with the previously mentioned brands, it needs a defect free, clean surface before application. It may be the most durable of all the three paints mentioned here, but it also needed quite a few layers in order to create a uniform, chromed surface, and to prevent the black undercoat from shining through. Again, the finish is not that different from Alclad II Chrome and the process is basically the same.

1.2.8 MOLOTOW LIQUID CHROME

Molotow Liquid Chrome is unlike the three paints mentioned above. First, it's not a modelling paint. As a matter of fact, it's not a paint at all. The available liquid version is a actually a refill for the Molotow Liquid Chrome markers. You can buy a couple of pen versions or pick up the refill itself depending on how you want to apply it. For some applications, use of the pen itself may be more suitable than actually spraying. The marker pen is a fantastic tool for

picking out fine details on a model. There are also plenty of videos on the internet showing how the use of Molotow can change a rough surface into one glossy super chromed mirror-like surface. Does it really work that good? I wish I could say yes, but, sadly…no, it does not.

The good thing about Molotow is that it doesn't require a glossy black undercoat. What it does require is a thick, initial layer of itself laid down. The heavy, wet first layer eventually levels out and forms a mirror-like surface. The first coat needs to be so thick, you need to virtually "pour" it on the surface with your airbrush, and this, of course, is not good at all. First, it's difficult to keep things under control with such a large amount of wet paint "sitting" on the part. It tends to run down and form puddles along the part edges. Second, it creates lines in the surfaces around the wet areas as they dry out, making it difficult to create a uniform layer of paint on the surface. Making a uniform layer on a large part, such as a

bumper or a fuel tank, is virtually impossible (and I've tried it multiple times). Furthermore, spraying such a heavy layer of paint means it is very likely that you will have some dust and other debris collect on the surface, which leads to another problem...the surface cannot be sanded or polished in any way. The heavy layer of paint needs days and/or weeks to dry, and even then it tends to be a bit sticky. The manner of application is exactly opposite of the way you would apply the very fine layers of Alclad. You can thin the original refill with a little bit of Mr.Color thinner, and it improves the behaviour of the paint slightly, but not in a significant way. While the use of Molotow Liquid Chrome on larger parts can lead to disaster, there is an array of parts where it can be used with far more acceptable results. Smaller parts such as an air horns, marker lights and other details can be sprayed without a glossy black under layer. Its quick, the results look virtually as good as Alclad or similar. The Molotow pens work great for hand painting small details such as the window trims, door handles, data plates, logos or interior details.

While not suitable for use on everything, and definitely not an easy paint to use, the Molotow Liquid Chrome can very useful for detailing some aspects in the building and detailing of your models. Molotow Liquid Chrome will do what other "Alclad type" paints can do on smaller parts, and it does it quickly and without the need for a black undercoat..

For the chrome-like surface there has always been one paint used and recommended worldwide and that is the Alclad II Chrome.

1.2.9 OTHER METALLIC PAINTS

There are several other metallic paints available on the market can be used to represent other types metallic finishes, such as brass, copper, steel or a generic burned exhaust metal. Most of these brands also offer aluminium paints, though the aluminium finish may look different than what you can achieve with the previously discussed products. Some can be as shiny as chrome when polished, others will be flat and greyish depending on the surface nature and maintenance. In order to obtain a highly polished aluminium finish, I suggest the use any of the chromed paints mentioned above (there is also the Alclad Polished aluminium available). Mr.Color Silver No.8 has always been my favourite for painting the typical, unpolished aluminium parts. Its pigment is so fine that the paint does not leave any visible surface texture unlike many of the other metallic paints available on the market.

Other paint products are available that are actually polishable paints which can be brushed or sprayed and later polished for that perfect, smooth finish. Gunze offers their Mr.Metal Color range of paints that can be polished with a fine cloth after spraying. A similar range of paints, that are spirit based,

For smaller corrections either Molotow Liquid Chrome or Agama metallic paints are very handy.

are made by Czech company Agama. These can be hand-painted or sprayed. When polished the paint surface is very convincing. I've been using them successfully on everything from the smallest little hand painted parts, to aluminium air tanks. Both manufacturers offer a variety of metal tones. Remember, many vehicle parts are made of steel. Don't forget that steel oxidizes quickly, so you don't typi-

cally see a natural "steel" colour on vehicles, as they quickly rust. Jet exhaust is great to spray over stainless exhaust pipes that tend to colorize when exposed to high temperatures. Copper may not be of use on model trucks, but brass can be used to make the yellow zinc plating used on many of the accessories, fittings, valves or polished brass parts on older vehicles.

1. The Alclad Chrome needs a very fine polishing after applicaton. Use a fine cloth and be very easy on the pressure as it is very easy to expose the black surface underneath.

2. Metallic parts does not necessarily mean high shine. When not maintained properly the aluminium rims easily get stained and loose their shine quickly.

3. For a matt effect, flat clear varnish was used over the original kit chrome followed by filters from black and yellow Tamiya clear coats.

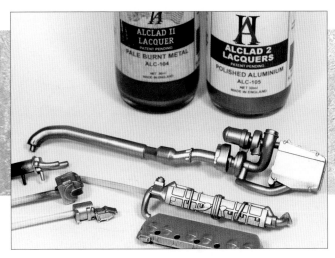

Alclad offers burnt metal tones for metallic parts exposed to high temperatures.

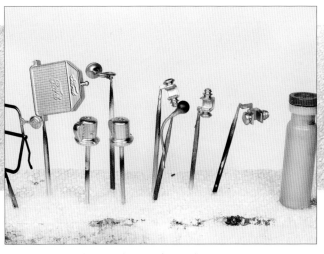

Brass is another typical material for antique vehicle parts but can also be used effectively to imitate the yellow zinc plating on modern vehicles.

Finally, it's also worth mentioning that there have been several other high-quality acrylic based metallics released lately, like Misson Models and Vallejo's Metal Color range.

SUMMARY

As you can see there is a wide variety of metallic paints available for plastic modellers, giving everyone a chance to choose a product that suits them. Never the less, painting chrome-like surfaces is still a challenging and demanding process, even with all the modern products available. Developing and maintaining a clean, precise building and painting techniques is still the way to go. The availability of these extraordinary paints, that allow the replication of different types of metallic finishes on truck models, is a gift to modellers as most vehicles come with all sorts of metallic components unpainted. Whether it's the wheels, fuel or air tanks, or just the fittings and small details you're painting, using these products adds a another level of authenticity and realism to the model, and brings our plastic creations closer to where we all want them to be…looking like the real thing. ■

metallics

washes & filters

1.3 WASHES & FILTERS

Before moving on, I'd like to quickly review these two basic techniques and make sure that you understand the differences between them as well as how they are to be applied. I've found that model builders are often confused when it comes to distinguishing between these terms, and as I will be using these techniques throughout the whole book, so it is important there is clarity. These two techniques are essential and useful tools for painting and weathering models.

A wash is an application of a highly thinned paint (70 - 80% of thinner) intended to highlight surface details, or add depth to panel lines around doors and other openings. It is meant to recreate shadows from which elevated details (such as bolt heads or rivets for example) stand out. In other words, it creates contrast and adds a more dramatic look to the surface of the model. The wash is applied so that it collects in corners, gaps and other surface recesses and should not cover the whole surface of the model. Black, dark grey, brown or generally darker versions of the original surface colours should be used when applying washes. Washes can also represent dirt or accumulated dust in such areas where surface debris tends to collect. In some instances brighter colours may be used as all sorts of dusts are suitable.

In contrast to a wash, a filter is meant to be applied over the whole model or a specific area (for example a panel) evenly to change its colour tone. The purpose is to alter the surface tones slightly, not dramatically, in order to add subtle colour variations. This is usually the first technique to start with when preparing the model surface for weathering. The paint should not collect around the surface details the way that a wash does. The paint used for filtering is usually thinned about 95 - 98 %, therefore the effect after application of one layer should be barely visible. It is usually necessary to repeat the process in same area until the desired effect is obtained.

What a wash and a filter have in common is that they should both be applied on a glossy or semi-gloss surface rather than on matt. The finer surfaces allow for a better control of the process and have limited paint adhesion. This allows for the gradual build-up of effects in steps.

1. Prior to any work with oils I always use a cardboard pallet to remove as much linseed oil as possible from the paint.

2. I use an aluminium palette for preparing and working with washes and filters.

3. A typical wash contains about 70 - 80 % thinner and looks very opaque on the palette.

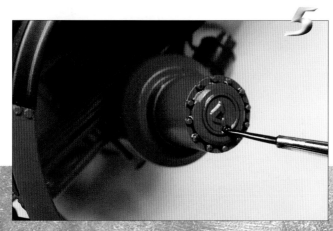

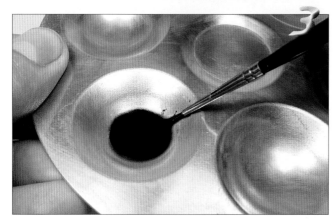

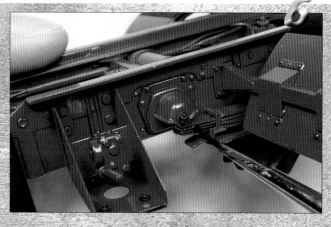

4. Some surface structures on plastic models such as different grooves or tight corners may lack contrast.

5. A dark (black or brown) wash is frequently used to add contrast.

6. Bolts, rivets, corners or leaf springs are all typical details that benefit from dark washes.

7. In contrast to dark washes, a light dust wash was used to highlight the tyre sidewall details on this example.

1. A filter contains about 95% thinner. It is less opaque than the wash.

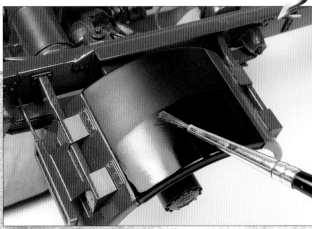

2. The first layer applied shows almost no effect, but repeated layers will gradually build up the result.

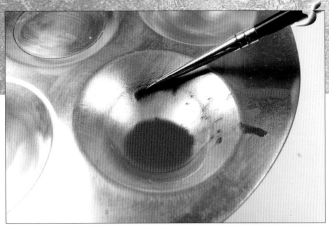

3. The brush movement shows that the filter is almost clear.

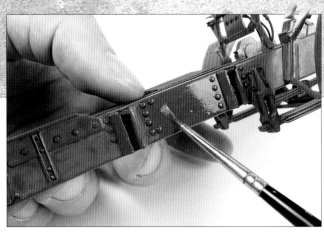

4. While the wash is meant to be applied into corners and around details mainly, the filter is applied on the entire surface and the key is to not let it collect around any details.

5. The Volvo frame treated with a black oil paint wash to highlight all the surface details.

6. The impact of the filters after a few layers have been applied and dried. The original red colour was shifted to orange, a typical effect seen on old PKS trucks, and all the aging plastic parts were shifted towards green a little.

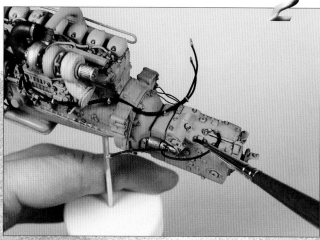

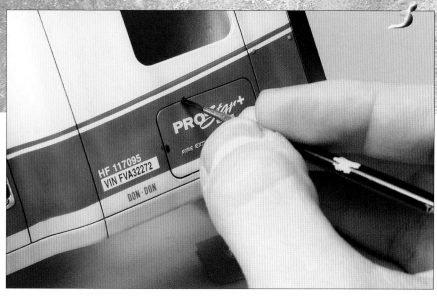

1. Light greyish dust filters can be used for fading the original paint and reducing its contrast to the surrounding components.

2. A dark wash is typically used to highlight bolt heads and rivets.

3. Panel lines can also be highlighted effectively with dark washes.

4. In some cases, the filter may also be used as a wash at the same time, as it imitates dirt accumulated in corners.

5. The grey on this Iveco frame has lost its dark tone over time. Applying a light grey filter is a great technique for adjusting the colour nuance on a weathered vehicle.

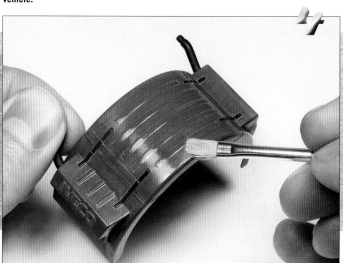

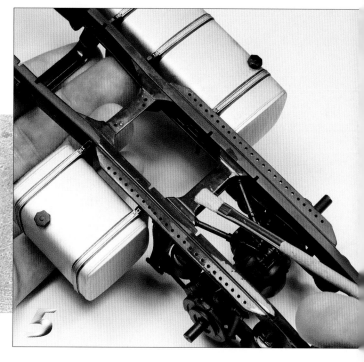

2 WORKING WITH PHOTO ETCH

Using photo-etched (PE) details is an effective way to improve the level of detail on your model. This section describes the tools and materials required.

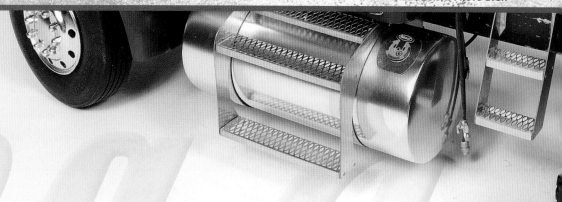

2.1 INTRODUCTION

Photo-etched (PE) parts are made of thin sheet metal (brass, stainless steel etc). The production technology is very precise and allows the reproduction of even the finest features that other technologies are not capable of. However, the material thickness is limited and is usually around 0.2mm. Any three-dimensional subjects built from PE parts therefore have to be made by bending/folding, which is the most common operation when working with this medium. Cutting the parts is not as easy as with plastic, but as the material thickness is relatively small, common tools such as knives or scissors can still be used. Painting PE is simple and does not require any special treatment, but for gluing, cyanoacrylate adhesives such as Superglue, or two-part epoxy glues, have to be used. As PE components are often very small, and the resulting sub-assemblies are quite delicate, the process is only really recommended to experienced model builders only (although we all have to start somewhere). Let's discuss the main characteristics of working with this medium.

2.1.1 TOOLS

Working with PE is different from working with plastic; you do not need any special tools for 95% of cases. All I use is: a solid pad, a sharp knife with strong blade, a metal ruler, small scissors and a wide choice of sanding equipment (sandpaper, sanding sticks and files. Is a bending tool necessary for working with PE parts? No, it is not. It can help in some instances, but you can live without it and so do I.

2.1.2 GLUING AND FILLING

Photo-etched parts are made of metal and therefore, normal glue for plastic models does not work. All the agents, both putties and glues for plastic, are based on melting the surfaces of the parts before joining them – but that is not the case for PE. There are three main substances I use: good cyanoacrylate glue (and debonder/remover) and an accelerator.

As for the glue I do not want to force you into buying one brand, but quality matters and all the adhesives I use are from Loctite. Its products are available worldwide so you should not have any problem in obtain them. I do not use just one glue, but usually different types for varying purposes. A standard liquid Loctite Super Glue for general purpo-

> *The production technology is very precise and allows the reproduction of even the finest features that other technologies are not capable of.*

1. This is a typical example of a PE set for truck models. It contains a painted dashboard to replace the kit decals, and it also features nickel plated parts to represent silver.

2. Etched parts are ideal for replicating thin sheet metal, grilles and mesh. These Peterbilt frame steps would never look as good in injection moulded plastic.

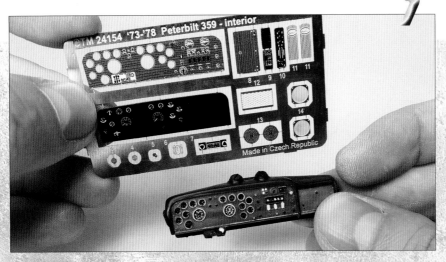

1. Hand painting vs. painted PE parts. Combining several layers of PE results in authentic details that can not be achieved by brush painting.

2. Three dimensional objects can also be made from PE to replace less detailed resin or plastic items.

se, a Power Easy (3g package), which gives you few more seconds before it hardens (and that is essential for working with fine parts you need to stick somewhere and have few extra seconds for perfect alignment) and Loctite 480 which, according to the company spec sheet is: "a rubber toughened adhesive with increased flexibility and peel strength, along with enhanced resistance to shock". It is great for both gluing and filling. It is not as brittle as standard Super Glue… and again gives you few more seconds for correcting alignment. It has one more positive feature not mentioned in the spec sheet: it is not clear but black. Therefore, you can clearly see where the glue is during the filling and sanding process, while the standard version is clear and not so easily visible.

A glue remover is a liquid that melts cyanoacrylate. It does not melt plastic, however, but it does melt all kinds of paints so be careful when working with this and do not use it on painted parts. I use if for removing any excess glue after gluing or filling PE parts, where sanding is not possible (tight corners) or would simply take too long. I employ it often when gluing complex PE assemblies where the contact surface is relatively small. To prevent the join from being brittle I usually apply a little more Super Glue than needed, to ensure the contact is robust and, once dry, I remove the excess glue using a fine brush (I use Microbrush applicators).

A cyanoacrylate accelerator, or 'kicker', is a liquid that hardens the glue immediately. The brand I know comes in a spray can. I can imagine your questions: Why should I use this when Super Glue hardens in a few seconds? Well, yes it does when applied correctly and in just a small amount. However, when using a glue as a form of putty you usually need to apply more than a small drop to fill the gap, and this may take more than a few seconds to harden. It may take ten minutes or more.

Once working on something I do not want to waste time like this, and I therefore use the accelerator for hardening even a thin layer of glue. Using, accelerator the glue dries instantly and you can start with sanding immediately.

Do I use any epoxy glue on PE parts? No, but there is no reason why epoxy would not work#. I use Super Glue for all work on PE, but I like to use epoxy elsewhere on models and it has its own qualities too.

A useful tip: store your cyano adhesives in a fridge. This will help the glue to last longer as all the reactions resulting in hardening the glue inside the original package are much slower at lower temperatures. Put the glue into the fridge every time you don't work with it.

2.1.3 CUTTING AND SANDING

As most PE parts are relatively thin you should not have any problem using standard (or just a slightly robust) scissors to cut the parts from the fret. It can be done with a knife on

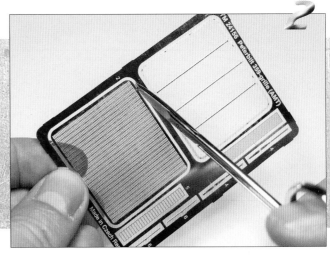

1. The best and most precise way of cutting PE parts out of the fret is to use a sharp knife on a solid surface.

2. A pair of fine scissors may also work very well.

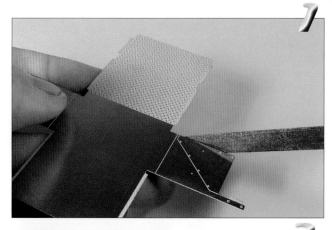

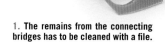

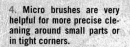

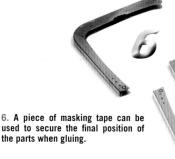

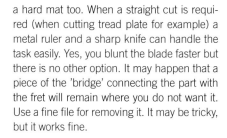

1. The remains from the connecting bridges has to be cleaned with a file.

2. The etched grille needs to be attached to the cab precisely. If done prior to painting the excess glue can be used to fill surrounding gaps.

3. Once dry the excess can be cleaned away with a piece of cloth and a glue remover.

4. Micro brushes are very helpful for more precise cleaning around small parts or in tight corners.

5. Handling of the smallest parts such as badges or lettering can be done with a toothpick and a small amount of Blu Tack.

6. A piece of masking tape can be used to secure the final position of the parts when gluing.

a hard mat too. When a straight cut is required (when cutting tread plate for example) a metal ruler and a sharp knife can handle the task easily. Yes, you blunt the blade faster but there is no other option. It may happen that a piece of the 'bridge' connecting the part with the fret will remain where you do not want it. Use a fine file for removing it. It may be tricky, but it works fine.

2.1.4 FINE PARTS HANDLING

Always remember that the tiniest PE components can easily fly away with just one breath and easily disappear in the 'black hole' un-

der your table. It is recommended to store all parts you do not need sealed in a box to prevent losing them. How should one pick them and fit into the right position on a model? Although there are many types and sizes of tweezers available, there is another way to manipulate even the smallest part, allowing you to apply glue on it and then attach it to the model's surface. All you need is a toothpick. The sharper the tip, the more accuracy is gained. Then you will need Tack-it (made by Faber-Castell but there are equivalents from other companies). When you roll a small ball of a few millimetres in diameter and stick it to

the end of the toothpick, you get a tool which you can use for lifting small parts. You can pick up a PE part with this tool, use another toothpick to apply a small amount of glue to the contact area and stick the part into the correct position on the model.

Using Tack-it for manipulation is useful, but sometimes you need to secure the part more strongly, especially during spraying, as it is quite easy to blow the part off the toothpick with an airbrush. To prevent this, I use Tamiya masking tape wrapped around a piece of wood or an old metal ruler. The trick is that the sticky surface of the tape should point out and remain free. This is where you can stick all the tiny bits such as letters or different logos and spray them comfortably.

2.1.5 BENDING AND ROLLING

As the etching technology allows working with plain flat sheets of limited thickness (mostly around 0.16-0.2mm), all results are as flat as paper. To make a three-dimensional subject, bending operations are needed. Working with PE parts this way is similar to building a paper/card model. All parts are printed on paper and it is up to the modeller to give them their final shape. It is the same with components; however, they are much more difficult to form as the metal properties are obviously different to those of paper. Yet still the basic principles remain the same. The parts can be bendt and rolled and three-dimensional objects can be created. For most parts in truck modelling a standard 90-degree bend is the most common, followed by similar operations resulting

in 45-degree bends etc. Rolling usually takes place when preparing exhaust heatshields.

On a PE part, you always find a pre-etched line wherever the bend operation should take place. Remember, this line should remain inside the corner once the bending operation is finished. It should form the inner edge and not an outer. If you place a PE part over a mat, the etched line should point upward and bending the part should also point upward. This means that the position of the pre-etched line indicates not just the right place for bending, but also a direction.

Now, bending the part simply means forcing one half towards a solid mat (using a metal ruler on a cutting mat, for example) while lifting up the second half of the part from the mat with a knife blade, which results in creating a sharp edge along the ruler so it not only provides the acting force that secures the part, but also provides an edge that defines where bending actually takes place. If you try to bend a part just in your hand, the result will probably be irregular and with a large radius, as there was no supporting edge for providing

a sharp bend. Pre-etched lines usually help considerably, so just minor force is necessary for bending. A sharp edge is created easily, and the result is clean and regular.

Rolling exhaust heat shields is the most common rolling operation on truck models. All you need for this is a tube of an appropriate diameter – usually smaller than the final diameter of the heat shield because the

Spraying small parts is actually quite easy. Just wrap a piece of inverted masking tape around a wooden block and stick the parts on it and then spray them carefully.

1. **Dedicated tools are available for folding PE parts. The first step is to fix the part along the bending line.**

2. **Once fixed properly, the part can be lifted with a solid knife.**

3. **Make sure the knife gets under the PE part as far as possible so that it bends along the edge of the tool and not elsewhere.**

4. **Alernatively, an ordinary metal ruler can be used, and I only use the special tool for the most tricky parts.**

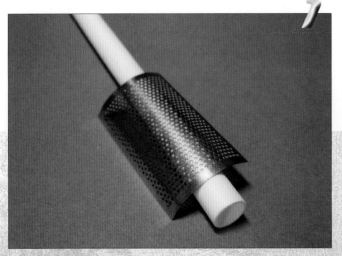

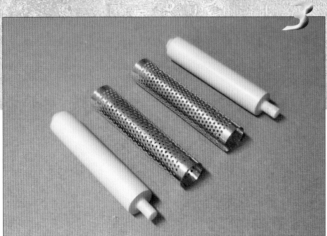

1. Rolling is a suitable operation for exhaust heatshields. Proceed with 3- 4 steps with pipes of different diameters.

2. The finished rolled part is on the left. The right hand one needs one more rolling on a small diameter pipe.

3. The finished heat shields. If the smallest rolling pipe is slightly smaller than the silencer diameter, they usually stay in place thanks to the spring-back force.

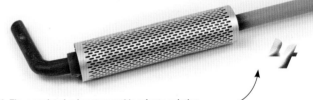

4. The completed exhaust assembly prior to painting.

part usually springs back somewhat, so you can't use 12mm tube for reaching a 12mm diameter. Starting from the flat PE part, slowly start pressing the heat shield over the tube and slowly wrap the etched part around it. It is useful to start with a tube of a larger diameter at first, let's say 20 or 30mm, to avoid sharp bends or edges on the heat shield that are difficult to remove, so a radius on the flat part can be generated slowly in small steps, avoiding any problems.

2.1.6 GLUING

After bending there are usually more parts to be connected. Usually you also need to stick a PE part to a plastic equivalent. Well, all the-se cases can be easily handled by one of the 'super' cyanoacrylate glues mentioned above. The final assembly is probably not as tough as a plastic version, and the joins may be brittle, but when you handle the parts with care you should have no problem.

There are two tips I would like to mention here: an application tool for Super Glue and a way of handling it.

How do you apply glue? Standard cement for plastic models comes with either a brush or a needle applicator, which help in applying the correct amount of glue exactly where you need it. But how should Super Glue be applied? Well, you can get it with a brush too but that's not very suitable for fine work, and most tube-style applicators do not enable gentle application either. So how should one apply a small amount of glue on a V8 logo that is just 3mm tall or an edge of a 0.16mm metal plate? A friend of mine showed me his custom-made tool for a glue application. I made it myself and I haven't used anything else since. It consists of a wooden stick (could be a toothpick or skewer) and a piece of wire or small diameter syringe needle. The wooden part forms a handle and the metal part glued into the handle is used to carry a small amount of glue. I machined a small flat area at the tip (I use a 1mm syringe needle), which allows me to carry the right amount of glue and place it anywhere I need. Of course, there will be

This means that the position of the pre-etched line indicates not just the right place for bending, but also a direction.

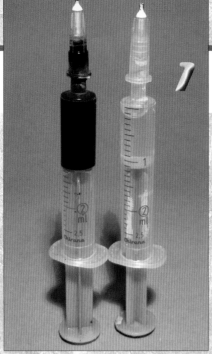

1. Super glue lasts for a long time if stored properly. I use small medical syringes for storing small amounts of glue at my workbench. The rest is kept cool in the fridge.

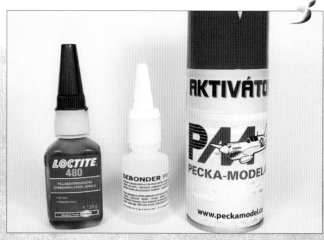

3. A perfect combination for gluing and filling PE parts. Black rubber-filled Loctite 480, a glue remover and a glue activator spray can.

2. I use a tool made of a piece of wire for a precise glue application. This works for any work on the model, not just the PE parts.

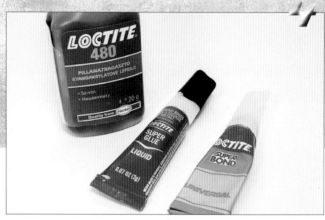

4. There are several types of super glue. The black 480 is sometimes hard to find but a regular liquid or gel Loctite can be found in a variety of shops and does a good job too.

more and more glue remaining on the tip of your tool. Use a lighter to remove it – all the remaining glue will burn, and your tool will be clean and ready for use again.

I do not use the original package for the glue I work with. When working with the glue regularly, the applicator usually gets covered with remaining adhesive, opening and closing gets more difficult, the cover does not seal properly and the glue inside the tube hardens. The only thing you can do is throw it away and buy a new bottle. I use a 2 ml medical syringe instead for a small amount of glue I work with. This means that every time I need glue, I fill a syringe with a small amount (not more than 1 ml, usually just 0.5 ml is enough for many days or weeks) and put the rest in the original tube into the fridge. I use a cap from a syringe needle to close the syringe and prevent the glue from hardening. When properly closed the glue in the syringe lasts for many weeks. Once you run out of it, you can fill the syringe from the

original tube again. Once the glue hardens in it, you just throw it away and fill a new one.

Now, if you remove the cap and push the plunger gently, a small drop of glue will appear on the syringe tip. It needs practice to get just the right size of drop. Once it's too big, it will spill out or if you push the plunger too fast, the glue will be blown out, covering everything around so don't try this while sitting on a new leather sofa! Use a piece of Tack-it mentioned before to ensure the syringe can stand upright on the table. Now it's secured and you can use the tool created in the previous step for precise glue application. Once you are done, just push back the plunger, which will suck all the glue back in (make sure you don't keep any air inside, just the glue) and you can refit the cap.

2.1.7 SOLDERING

Soldering PE is still somewhat unexplored for me. I have never needed this method, as I always managed fine enough with Su-

per Glue. Being responsible for development and testing of many CTM products, I can't say, however, I haven't seen complex tasks or tricky PE assembly. In any case, we at CTM always tried to ensure you do not need any special tools.

There are cases, however, where soldering is beneficial and makes one's life significantly easier. In general, this is with larger assemblies or parts that are required to withstand stress during the model assembly or transportation. A friend of mine, a great modeller who stands behind A&N Model Trucks, Andrey Myakotkin, has always highlighted the importance of soldering. Many of his truck kits use photo-etched frames that are precise replicas of the real thing. As the frame is the backbone of the whole model, it must be strong enough to carry all the parts combined. Transporting models to shows and exhibitions, or just handling during the assembly, may both create severe conditions that Super Glue simply cannot cope with. Here, and it is just one

1. A PE grille to replace the plastic part in the Italeri MAN kit. The mesh is a smart design and is just one layer but still it looks three dimensional.

2. Even the finest etched signs or plates can be painted. These were first sprayed black, followed by either white or yellow that was carefully sanded away from the lettering.

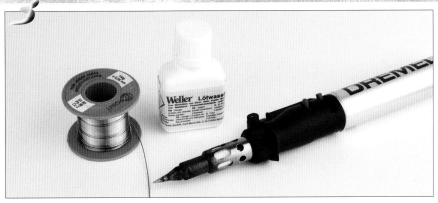

3. A basic set-up for soldering: soldering wire, soldering fluid and a soldering iron. This iron is gas driven but the electric heated ones are more typical.

of many other applications, soldering does much better than any other joining process.

For soldering you need a soldering 'iron', solder and a soldering acid for treating PE parts before application of solder. You can find many online guides for this and I can recommend those directly made by Andrej, showing useful examples of building model trucks. Search youtube for A&N Model Trucks channel (How to solder photo-etched parts).

2.1.8 FILLING

I have already mentioned that standard putty for plastic cannot be used when working with PE parts. However sometimes it is important to hide a join to obtain a smooth surface, so filling is needed. Well, as the Super Glue adheres to the metal surface much better than any putty, there is no reason for not using it as filler. Just apply enough glue in the gap, on the edge or simply anywhere you need it, apply accelerator and remove the excess either with sanding or glue remover. There is nothing special about filling PE parts. Do it the

same way as you do when working with resin or plastic. The only difference may be the fact that the parts are usually small and fine, and that the assembly is delicate.

2.1.9 PAINTING

Painting metal parts does not represent anything special compared to painting other parts. You should be careful when handling painted PE as the paint usually does not adhere to metal as well as plastic, so is prone to damage. I recommend using primer beforehand, as it helps with paint adhesion, but I recommend that for any kind of parts anyway.

The only more advanced approach is required when painting fine surface structures on various logos or plates. You can use a brush and try and paint all the details by hand, but there is another way. A common combination is a generic truck badge that should consist of silver letters and numbers and black background. For this reason, many PE parts are nickel silver, so basically just a black background should be painted. To do this, spray

the part with a fine black coat. In the next step, remove the paint from the raised areas by careful sanding. Use either very fine abrasive paper or a sanding stick, and be careful as the silver nickel surface on the brass can be damaged with sanding. Now you have a black background with all the raised details in the native metal surface. It is easy and very effective.

How about a TIR plate, for example, which needs the letters in black and not silver? In case you want the elevated details in a different colour, spray a coat of the one particular shade over the part first. Make sure the coat is nicely thick and let it dry long enough to harden properly. Once white and dry you can now apply the second, blue colour. Unlike the previous coat, apply just a very thin layer. Once dry, you can again remove the blue by sanding it away, leaving the lower white layer untouched. It needs practice, but with patience this technique can be used efficiently. ∎

3 BUILDING A FRAI

A frame is an elementary structural member of a model that holds all the individual components together, but its details are usually not discussed that often within the truck modelling community.

E FROM SCRATCH

3.1 INTRODUCTION

It is understandable that with many kits you just follow the instructions and glue the frame rails and cross members together without any need to talk about what you are doing. The importance of frames, working with them and constructing them comes into play when you try to venture beyond out-of-box builds – and either modify a frame or scratch-build your own. The need for this comes quite often as there are plenty of resin cabs, as well as axle and suspension kits that call for modifications. But when it comes to it, are you able to build your own frame?

I decided to include a short chapter about building frames, mainly because I appreciate the liberating feeling that comes with the ability to build anything you need without being dependent on what Italeri and AMT may have manufactured. Being able to scratch-build your frame is a must, and it is not as demanding a task as it might seem, because much of the hard work can be done with Evergreen or Plastruct profiles, and resin/photo-etched metal accessories. This chapter will give you a hint of how to do it.

Modifying a frame is usually needed when a wheelbase or suspension conversion takes place. There is an existing frame you have, but you need to make it longer or shorter or maybe modify some cross members. As there is guidance present in the existing frame you can either use a donor kit as a source for a piece of an appropriately sized frame rail, with which to lengthen your existing item, or you can use strips of plastic card of a suitable thickness (+ / - 1mm) to create the extension. Usually additional strip is added inside such a frame rail for reinforcement, as the joints may be brittle and are easy to break. When a longer extension is needed there are usually two ways to go. Either to use two frame rails from as many kits and combine them into one, or just scratch-build the whole thing yourself.

An essential beginning of scratch-building your own frame is to have some dimensions or a drawing. You need to know the basic

> *I appreciate the liberating feeling that comes with the ability to build anything you need without being dependent on what Italeri and AMT may have manufactured.*

measurements and shapes of both the frame rails and crossmembers. In the end, the major dimensions are three values: the frame rail length and height and the frame width. Knowing these values and using a reasonable wall thickness for the frame rail vertical and horizontal sections will define the rest, mainly crossmember width and height. I have seen many modellers trying to get a reasonably sized profile for the frame rails (which they ne-

1. **A 1950s Peterbilt chassis featuring a pair of aluminium frame rails and cast aluminium main suspension crossmembers.**

2. **Note the frame rail thickness. It is not very far from how some of the frames are replicated in the AMT kits.**

3. **A modern Scania steel frame with stamped steel crossmembers. Note how thin the material is compared to the aluminium frame.**

A Volvo F89-32 frame. The frame rails are straight and unlike the modern frames each of the holes has its purpose.

ver found), but the fact is, the easiest way is to build your own is from sheet and strip. The vertical web section should be thick enough to carry the model's weight so I would not choose thinner than 1mm. The horizontal sections are not so important, and to achieve realistic thickness I usually make the lower flange 0.5 or 1mm, but the upper just 0.3 or 0.5mm to replicate a relatively thin steel sheet (unless the frame is made of aluminium).

Cutting a piece of 1mm sheet that is 10mm high and some 300 mm long is something that an average modeller should be capable of. Work slowly, ensuring the cuts are perpendicular and have clean edges. The top and bottom flanges can effectively be made of Evergreen strip No.117 (0.38 x 4.mm) or 127

(0.5 x 4.0 mm). For attaching flanges to the web, use a regular glue for plastic models and make sure the web and flange are perfectly perpendicular. Once dry, the joins on the outer side of the rail need filling and sanding, for which I often use black superglue to speed up the process. Make sure you also sand the outer frame rail edges, as the real examples are also rounded.

With the frame rails completed, crossmembers will be required. Making your own is basically the same as making the frame rails – an analogical process can be used, just the required shape may be more complex. The cross members behind the transmission usually have a curved bottom flange to provide enough clearance for the prop shaft. When

scratch-building, I usually make both my own rails and cross members, but when I do not want to spend so much time on that I often go to my spares box and find something of a similar size and shape. There is also a KFS TQ88 CNC milled plastic frame. I used it on the Peterbilt 350 frame and the leftover crossmembers were employed on the GMC Cannonball frame. In addition to these, leftover photo-etched cross members were used on the Cannonball, enhancing the area behind the cab with pleasingly thin sheet metal parts.

I have already mentioned all the multiple ways of making bolts and rivets on truck models. On the frames, just like anywhere else on heavy vehicles, bolts and rivets are requi-

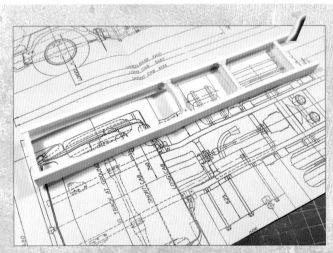

1. A drawing is an absolute must for a precise scratch-building work. This gives you all the important information about the parts' sizes and positions.

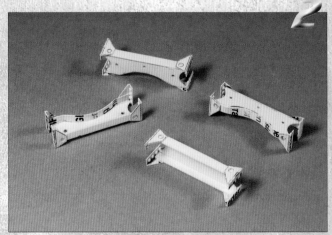

2. The crossmembers are usually more complex then the rails themselves. You can build your own or save time and use them from your spares box.

1. Cut the frame rail vertical sections from a 1 mm sheet with a sharp new scalpel blade for increased precision.

2. Remove any imperfections by sanding to reduce the need for filling in the next step.

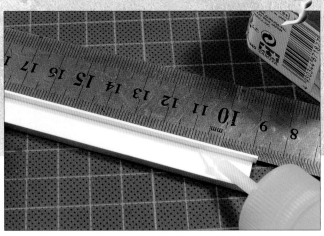

3. The frame horizontal sections were made from Evergreen strip, glued with thin plastic cement to attach them to the vertical section.

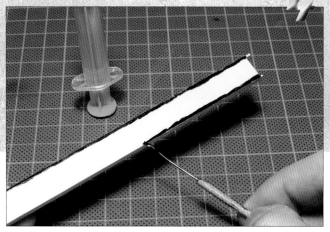

4. I like to use black super glue for filling, applied along the length of the joins.

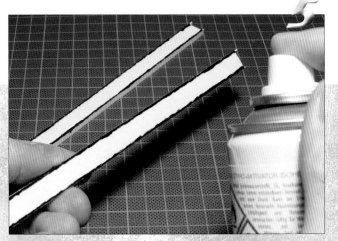

5. Super glue activator will speed up the procces.

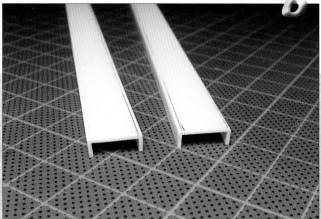

6. The finished rails. Note the black glue fills the gaps. The joins were sanded smooth.

I often use Locktite black super glue to speed up the process.

red, and these may come either from aftermarket resin or plastic sets – or can be made by cutting rounded and hexagon Plastruct rods, or from styrene sheet using circular or hexagonal punch-and-die sets.

The welds, if needed, can either be sourced from the CTM PE set or fashioned from either plastic rod melted with modelling glue (and moulded with a scalpel blade) or directly from modelling putty such as Miliput or Magic Sculp.

Once the frame is assembled (make sure the crossmembers and rails are precisely perpendicular) and detailed, the axles and suspension follow. While the rear axle and suspension is often quite visible and its details are important, the front axle, with its steering and suspension on any model can basically come from any suitable donor kit. If there is none available, I can only recommend the KFS TQMT-4 white metal front axle, strong enough to carry any heavy resin cab and re-

lated parts. The rear axles are sometimes not so easy to solve as the different suspension systems have their distinctive features (Hendrickson, Kenworth torsion bars…) and are obvious on a model, but for generic purposes on a vehicle with standard leaf springs and single drive axle, I usually use a resin copy of the parts from the Heller Scania LB 141 kits. Of course, the most typical suspension sets and axles are often available by various aftermarket suppliers. ■

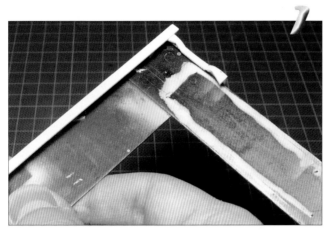

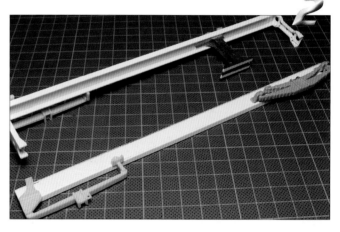

1. When adding crossmembers to the side rail, make sure everything is perfectly perpendicular.

2. I usually attach all the crossmembers to one rail and then add the second rail. The suspension comes from the spares box too.

3. The robust white metal axles made by KFS and M&G are a great help for scratch-building vehicles.

4. I also use resin bolts and rivets for detailing the crossmembers.

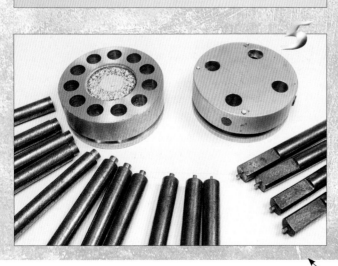

5. Different punch and die sets will help you create all the necessary bolts and rivets.

1. Using the punch and die sets is quick and easy.

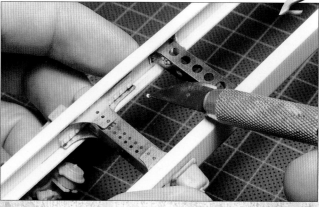

2. I often use the tip of a scalpel blade to place all the bolt heads in their position.

3. The bolts attaching the crossmember to the frame rail are visible both on the inside and outside of the frame.

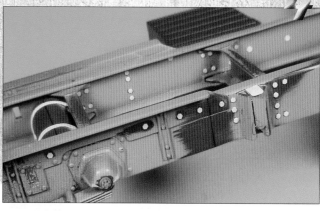

4. Knowing how to make bolts is handy for detailing kit frames too as they are usually missing.

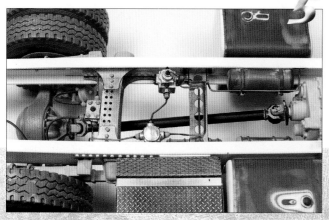

5. Adding the air valves and plumbing does not differ from detailing a kit frame.

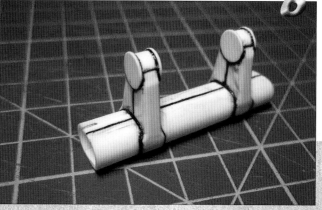

6. For weld seams, I usually use a strectched sprue (as when making an antenna), melt it with glue and shape the bead with a scalpel blade.

7. Working with frames does not necessarily mean scratch-building. On this Volvo F12 the frame was shortened to represent the wheelbase of 3600 mm.

REFERENCE GALLERY

This chapter is a visual guide to the weathering that real trucks are exposed to daily. Even trucks that are frequently washed and maintained will inevitably show signs of wear and tear.

4.1 INTRODUCTION

Model weathering is a popular discipline. There are many books and articles dedicated solely to this topic, but mostly this has been demonstrated on 1/35 scale models. That scale is large enough, however, that using the same techniques on 1/24 or 1/25 scale subjects is barely any different. However, I still meet modellers who do not understand the basic principles.

One of the fundamental requirements for weathering a model successfully is the understanding of the techniques themselves, but also the mechanisms of formation on the real vehicles. Do not underestimate this part of the process; look at a real truck closely and see how the dust, dirt and rust collects and how the signs of wear appear, where and why. There is a natural balance between all the weathering effects found on the vehicle at one time (how much rust, grease, dirt and where) and keeping it on a realistic level. Actual vehicles should always be observed for reference.

Advanced weathering (going further than adding a little grease on the truck's fifth wheel) means going deeper into many techniques and special paints (such as oils). It needs time to understand, learn and practice. Don't expect to gain all the skills overnight and don't think you can perform convincing weathering of a truck model in an hour. Good and detailed weathering on a truck model can easily be half of the whole model's build time.

This chapter is divided into three sub-sections, each dealing with its own topic.

4.2 THE 5TH WHEEL   PAGE 36

Weathering a 5th wheel is one of the elementary steps of the weathering process, and it provides the model with an eye catching detail.

4.3 RUST & CHIPPING   PAGE 38

Rust is an important feature, even on less weathered models, and can be carried out in many different styles.

4.4 DUST & DIRT   PAGE 44

Regardless of a vehicle's age or mechanical state, it will inevitably be covered with dust and dirt to various extent after just a very short service period.

4.2 THE 5TH WHEEL

Weathering a fifth wheel is the most elementary weathering task a model truck builder runs into. Even when building a model of a clean but working truck the fifth wheel can be seen and it is by its very nature dirty with grease. This grease is spread around the area outside of the working fifth wheel surfaces where it stays and collects dust and dirt. This can be seen on almost all vehicles except for those with special aluminium or Teflon plated fifth wheels. Different truck shows are usually a good occasion to see it live and take some pictures as most vehicles attend the show without a trailer and with the fifth wheel nicely exposed. In general, they look quite same but

there are differences between the amounts of grease applied, its age and colour variations. On the modelling side, the process is quite simple and straightforward.

The typical grease and dirt colour for this varies from black to very dark brown and I use oil paints for this exclusively. The reason is that the oil paint can be easily used to build a thin layer and create a realistic surface structure. I used to apply it directly from the tube in the past but I have learned the benefit of applying the paint to a cardboard palette first to remove the excess oil in the paint (the more oil the longer the paint dries), let it there for a few hours (or even a day) and apply when the paint already starts to dry. I usually

use an old flat brush to apply the paint and create the typical ribbed structure of the grease created by a trailer sliding down from the fifth wheel top. The drier the oil paint the older the look of the grease. If needed the result can be sealed with a varnish.

1. Freshly applied grease on the 5th wheel of a GMC Astro tractor. Note the grooves on the 5th wheel plate. Their purpose is to keep some spare grease and distribute it slowly over the contact surfaces during their mutual motion.

2. Heavy grease deposits on a 5th wheel of what seems to be a hard working truck, but it is actually a Volvo G88 oldtimer. Note how the excess grease "flows" towards the rear end of the 5th wheel plate.

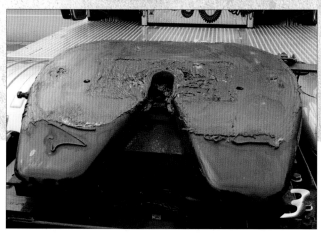

1. Note how the grease is pushed out in all directions by the contact between the plate and the trailer and how the greasy surface collects dust.

2. As the trailer slides down from the fifth wheel all the grooves are filled with the grease and the surface appears to be completely flat. Note the drying old grease, full of dust, at the tail end of the plate.

3. The modern 5th wheels do not need a lot of grease to perform properly. Note the fresh red grease on the tail section and the locking mechanism.

4. Not just the top surface but also the jaw and wedge mechanism need a proper lubrication and is always covered with heavy grease.

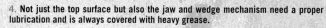

TECH-TIP
SEE HOW IT'S DONE
page 118

4.3 RUST & CHIPPING

Rust is an important weathering chapter. The specific rust tone depends on many aspects (the material, the environment, time of exposure) and is driven by natural laws. Therefore, different vehicle components on which rust develops vary and are rather specific. Fresh rust looks different to old rust. Rust on a turbocharger o exhaust manifold (where it is exposed to high temperatures) may look diffe-

rent to that found on the vehicle frame, and so on. The way a vehicle is operated may define what rust on the exhaust manifold looks like. Not speaking of the vehicle age or mileage of course. The tendency to form rust streaks on bodywork is affected by how frequently the vehicle is washed. Rust is always a colour variation, so it is about combining more tones.

Emulating chipped paint and scratches has become a very popular part of weathering, ad-

ding another level to the model's authenticity. While dust, mud and dirt represent vehicle fouling, chipped paint and scratches are a sign of a physical wear of the vehicle and its components, which may differ significantly in intensity from just the first signs of mechanical damage on a relatively new vehicle, to multiple paint layers and rust peeling off an old vehicle that has been repainted many times.

1. The exhaust rust has a typical structure with bright areas and dark contrasting spots.

2. Note how the colour of the turbine scroll exposed to high temperatures is in a brigh pinkish colour.

1. A relatively new Volvo engine showing no signs of weathering except for the exhaust manifold with a fine speckled texture.

2. This Gardner engine was obviously painted in different colours during its service life. Note how the chipped paint reveals another layer underneath while other chips go all the way down to the metal. Note also the dull grey aluminium on the rocker cover.

3. Chips and rust go together. Chips exposing the metal come first, and rust does the rest. Note how the rust have turned the yellow areas to orange over the years.

4. A beautiful example of vertical rust streaks and rain marks coming from the old chipped areas.

5. The paint peels away around large chips and the peeling paint appears brighter than the paint surrounding it. This is a typical example why hand painted chips are often painted in two layers - the inside rust and bright paint around it.

page 136

☼ TECH-TIP
SEE HOW IT'S DONE

page 95

TRUCK MODELLING

1. Even the smallest chips can cause subtle rust streaks if the vehicle is not washed regularly.

2. Long and narrow horizontal scratches are typical for bumpers. Again, the rust streaks have discoloured the paint on this aging truck.

3. Steel and aluminum. Note how the rust slowly eats the steel part bolted on the aluminium trailer side and affects its surrounding.

4. The small chips grow bigger over the years as the rust spreads underneath the paint that starts peeling away. Once again, note how the peeling paint around the chips appear brighter.

5. In this case, the water probably collected behind the lifted paint and created that bright rust edge along the lower edge of the large rusted area. Note also the colour and size of the streaks. This truck must have been sitting outside for years.

TECH-TIP
SEE HOW IT'S DONE
page 148

1. This 1963 Ford F600 mobile sheller truck may not look so tired from a distance but the next few close-up photos reveal a combination of age and wear. Note that the paint is still glossy however.

2. This is how it starts. There are no large chips but many small ones. Some are relatively new, and the older ones are surrounded by light surface rust.

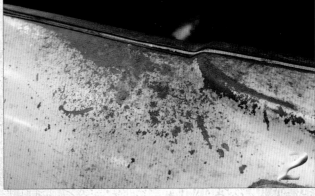

3. The window edge. The driver must have touched this part a thousand times when opening and closing the door, and the paint was slowly worn from the exposed edges over the years.

4. The handle is shining bright while the door edge has all the paint worn out and the metal is exposed. Note that the steel is polished and has no tendency to rust.

5. The bottom corner of the door is one of the first areas where severe rust appears. The rust already created a few small holes in the bodywork.

Rust & chipping

41

1. The F600 cab step shows how the bright green have been worn to reveal the coat of red underneath. The majority of the chips expose the bare metal however.

2. The white bumper also shows some fine rusty scratches. Note the fine dots on the bodywork, most likely caused by stone impacts when driving on gravel roads.

3. More severe impacts are evident as well, and the paint has been chipped away completely. Once again, note the little dots of chipped paint versus the relatively intact aluminium on the grille.

4. Exposed edges are always subjcted to heavier chipping. The sharp edge on the front mudguard has been worn regularly along its whole length for many years.

5. On this example, however, there are no evident sharp chips or scratches. In contrary, the paint on this Volvo N88 was faded by bright sun and once the paint was too thin, the corrosion started slowly.

6. The Volvo looks completely different compared to the F600 Ford. While the wear on the Ford is just a sign of an intense use, most of the effect on the Volvo happened when the vehicle was exposed to the weather.

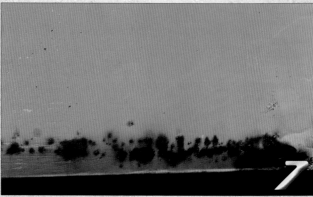

7. The bottom edge of the door. The water creeps in between the sheet metal parts and the corrosion starts inside. Over time it eats through the steel and paint and creates small rust bubbles.

Rust & chipping

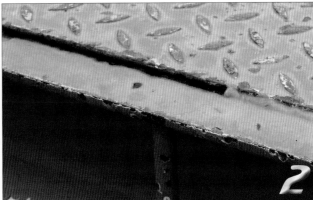

1. It is all in the details. This fuel tank shows no signs of heavy wear but the paint is already flat and there are many smaller chips on the edges.

2. The initial chips are small and start slowly on the exposed edges such as those on this low loader. Note that a white primer and a previous layer of grey paint are revealed in the chips too.

3. The end of this Volvo F12 frame rail was scratched repeatedly while attaching the trailer. Some scratches just reveal the bright primer, and others go through the paint completely.

4. More bumper chips and scratches. Some expose the orange underneath the black stripes, while others go through to the bare metal and are relatively fresh as there is no visible rust in them yet.

5. Contrasting chips in the red paint on the fuel tank that was originally black. Note that with the large chips a large amout of smaller ones is present.

6. The frame rail edges and the edges of the crossmember holes are areas where the rust appears first.

Have a closer look at page 130

...at page 130

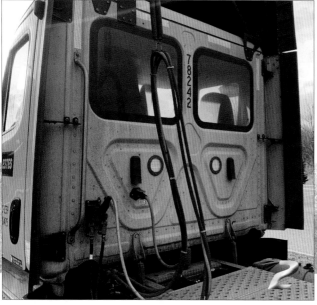

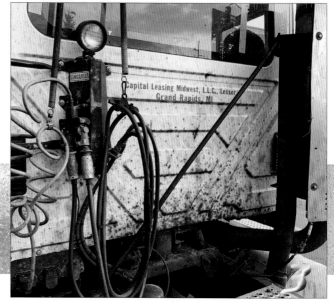

4.4 DUST & DIRT

Dust and dirt in various forms represent another layer of weathering that can be added to the model, regardless of the vehicle's mechanical state. Either new or old, rusty or freshly painted, both can be dirty from wheels to roof. Let us say there are three main sources of dirt.

The basic example signifies generic dust and dirt present everywhere. Just like you drive a vehicle on a regular road in the rain. Once your vehicle gets dry you easily see that it is no longer clean, and if you let the layers collect over a longer period, they tend to form a greyish coat all over the vehicle, including windows. As it builds up, it tends to collect more and more dirt and dust, forms rain marks and eventually gets removed from the parts of bodywork you touch regularly, such as door or trunk edges and so on. When using wipers, the layers are removed, and this creates the typical wiper traces on the windscreen.

The second source involves harsh conditions, such as driving off the highway on dirt roads, in mud or dust for example. This is a source of more intense earth-coloured dirt deposits and layers. It could be sand, earth, mud or any other colour tone related to the environment where the vehicle operates. It can also be related to the type of load the vehicle is carrying, especially in the case of dump trucks, garbage trucks or similar machines.

The third source of pollution embraces stains, deposits or leaks of all vehicle fluids – especially oil, grease and fuel. Grease spreads all over the engine, transmission and drive axles, as well as all manually lubricated areas such as pins, U-joints and fifth wheels. Fuel spills traditionally occur around the tank filling necks, soaking into the generic dust and dirt and hastening the build-up of dirt in this dampened area.

1. A hard working Western Star. The aluminium on the truck is all but shiny and the rubber on the tyres is barely visible under the dirt.

2. The cab rear walls are often the most weathered part of vehicle bodywork. The dust and dirt usually accumulates behind the fairings first.

3. A typical effect seen on the cab rear walls are the heavy oil and grease deposits from the drive train, especially the u-joints.

4. The catwalks are often dirty from the excess 5th wheel grease.

5. Heavy winch trucks are rarely clean. A mix of rust, dust and dirt is present all over the entire vehicle.

1. Heavy leaks, rain marks and dust are all evident on the surface of this 20ft container tank.

2. Note the heavy vertical streaks on this trailer door. It hasn't been washed for a while and the heavy rust on the bumper says a lot about its hard life.

3. Chrome is not necessarily polished and shiny. Note the greasy stains, most likely from a U-joint lube.

1. Light dust is more common than heavy and often look like bright filters over the lower vehicle areas, wheels, rims and fuel tanks. Note the large spots and stains over the battery box, fuel tank and the sleeper.

2. Comparing to picture above the dust on this 389 Peterbilt is a lot more uniform. On a model, this type of dirt can be achieved with an airbrush.

3. The heavy dust layer on this pick-up have been worn off the door where the driver has touched it frequently. Also note the darker tone of the dry mud splatter behind the wheel.

1. Fresh mud covers the side wall of this tyre, but the thread is much cleaner.

2. A good example of dry mud. Note how the thread is almost clean from the friction against the dry road.

3. This image illustrates lighter mud. On a model, finer splatters can be done with speckling, or brush painted.

4. Heavy dust on the dump truck rear axles accumulated after driving in a sand pit.

5. Dry and heavy mud deposits all over the front axle and suspension. Note the different colour tones of the mud.

6. A tandem axle suspension of a heavy dump truck working in a sand pit. The contrast between the wet and dry areas are evident.

7. The inside areas of the frames on highway trucks are often dirty from light grey or brown dust deposits.

1. Note the heavy mud splatters on the air tanks, from the front wheel.

2. A nice contrast between dark fuel stains around the filling cap and brighter dirt stains all over the tank. The dirt is not uniform and the individual stains and splatters are clearly visible.

3. Bright vertical streaks creates a nice effect on darker surfaces.

4. The fuel tanks easily gets dirty with fuel stains that in turn collect dirt and create a dark wet area around the lid.

5. A toolbox on a crane truck covered with oil stains, probably leaking from the hydraulic high pressure circuit nearby.

TECH-TIP
SEE HOW IT'S DONE
page 140

Dust & dirt

5 CAB INTERIORS

There is something special about building and detailing interiors. The feeling when you look inside someone's model cab and think 'that's so real' is very similar to seeing a detailed engine or a good paint job.

5.1 INTRODUCTION

I really enjoy when the upholstery is authentically replicated, when all the controls, levers and pedals are in place, when there is clear plastic applied over all the gauges and when I see the everyday junk that drivers need, which brings a cab interior into life. Interiors are simply models on their own and they represent a good portion of the work that goes into many kit projects.

It's because of all the different materials used inside a cab – leather, wood, textiles – that they may need special attention and different techniques to represent them convincingly. Patience and care play their part too, as many interior parts, especially the dashboard details, are very fine and delicate.

Upgrading a dashboard can be a straightforward task if there is a suitable PE set, perhaps even pre-painted. In other cases, however, serious detailing and scratch-buil-

ding may be required if the out-of-box interior is not good enough and there are no aftermarket sets available.

5.2 THE INTERIOR STRUCTURE

Model interiors mostly consist of similar parts, but the assembly sequence can be different and there are two basic groups into which 95% of kits fall. One is when the interior is assembled into an integral shell, around which the cab's external panels are built. With the

other solution, the cab internal walls are a part of the cab shell and just the floor is inserted. In general, assembling the exterior panels around the finished interior is not always

1. A typical Italeri interior consists of floor, walls and dashboard that can be assembled separately.

2. The Heller Scania cab assembly is very specific and there is no other way than to assemble it separated from the individual panels after painting.

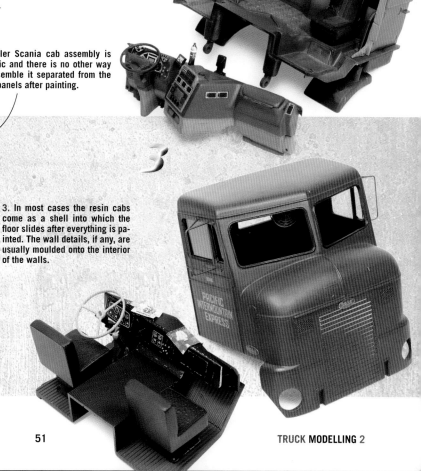

3. In most cases the resin cabs come as a shell into which the floor slides after everything is painted. The wall details, if any, are usually moulded onto the interior of the walls.

convenient as it requires a different approach when painting the exterior, which is usually conducted in one piece.

A generic interior comprises a floor plate (which sometimes comes together with lower side walls and door panels in the form of a tub – typical for AMT kits) to which seats on their mounts, and the gearstick are attached. As a separate part the dashboard comes fitted with a steering column and pedals (if they are not on the floor). Bunks and all the surrounding wall and roof panels follow. The interior walls may also be moulded as a part of the cab outer walls, or it may be that some interior panels are missing completely. While some cabs come with a complete interior, other examples and sleepers may come entirely empty. The seatbelts are always missing.

The truth is that often, only a small percentage of the interior is visible on the finished model. There are some exceptions; for example some Revell kits, which come with opening cab doors and removable roofs that afford a better view of the inside. However, it does sometimes mean toy-like features, which of course is undesirable. I always like to detail the cab interior with extras, but I often do it only to take photographs of it, as after the cab is assembled nobody will ever see what is behind the seats and all other details will disappear. What often remains visible are the seats, dashboard, the controls, and the steering wheel. Additional details such as cab curtains or paraphernalia placed all around can be seen too if placed cleverly.

5.3 UPHOLSTERY & CARPETING

The upholstery represents a large percentage of the interior surfaces. It is not only the seats and door panels but also all the walls, bunks, and a fair portion of the floor. Especially when the pattern or colour is distinctive it should be represented accurately, and this makes upholstery quite an important topic. Real interiors are made of soft materials and

1- 5. For the flocking, apply a fine layer of a white glue over the part and use a fine kitchen strainer to distribute the flocking over the part evenly. The result is a fine, soft looking plush-like surface.

6. For irregular textures that are to be painted and weathered, a thinned Tamiya putty applied with an old brush is one of the alternatives.

7. The typical padded texture can be made from styrene sheets available from H.A. Models from Denmark.

8. If a more complex surface has to be covered, the Miliput Superfine White putty can be used for moulding any type of structure.

9. The Danish plush in the picture is a dedicated sticker made for truck modellers.

Padded upholstery is common on modern European custom trucks.

More complex and colourful patterns can be made with decals or self adhesive stickers.

for obvious reasons they rarely look authentic when moulded in styrene.

There are two different sides of this coin though, as there are extremely talented modellers who can mimic anything with paint, so that it looks like a soft cushion and textile surface. Others will always prefer using self-adhesive carpets, real textiles or at least flocking for making the upholstery look real in their eyes. Some kits have the upholstery and seat, or floor structure moulded so well that it only needs a little painting to create a

good result (some old AMT kits for example, the Italeri Iveco TurboStar or the International Prostar from Moebius), but other kits may need enhancement. I have never been keen on self-adhesive carpets as they are too much out of scale in my opinion – neither do they replicate uneven surfaces convincingly. The real textile may also be a problem because the structure of the fabric can easily be seen, and the cloth is also usually quite hard to wrap around curved surfaces. Flocking made for car modellers may look finer if you want to

differ and stay away from chunky plastic seats and bunks. I gave it a chance on a couple of models in this book for demonstration purposes, but I do not think the final results are too authentic.

Flocking is a powder that consists of short textile fibres soft enough to perform like a pigment dust. It creates a plush-like texture when applied to any surface. Applying flocking is rather simple. The first step is to spray the part with a colour that is as close to the flocking as possible. This will limit the basic

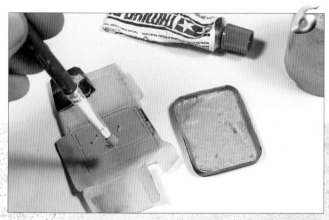

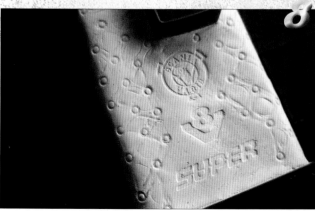

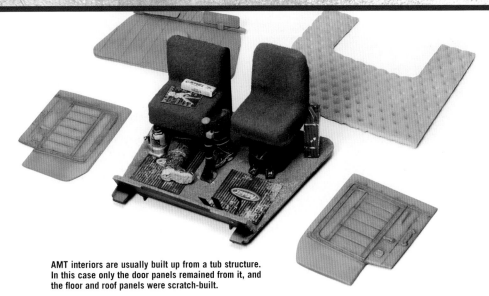

AMT interiors are usually built up from a tub structure. In this case only the door panels remained from it, and the floor and roof panels were scratch-built.

surface 'shining' through the flocking, and it will mean that fewer layers of flocking will be needed. Once painted appropriately, white glue has to be applied all over the part where the flocking needs to sit. While the glue is still wet, the flocking is loaded into a fine strainer and applied all over the glue. The fibres collect over the surface and are captured by the glue. Some fall off and the first layer may not be opaque enough (this is there where the appropriate colour underneath comes into play) so the process may have to be repeated, but two layers are often enough.

A cheap source of fine structure cloth can be found in paper tissues. These can be applied over a seat or bunk surface, softened and fixed with water and a little white glue. Painted paper tissue may also be used to make decent soft cab curtains.

A similar effect of enhancing a part surface with a texture is applying a thinned putty or primer with a brush, in a similar manner to when armour modellers replicate a cast steel part structure. It is quick and easy, and this finish will suitably accept further oil paint effects.

I like to make my own model curtains and blankets but have become tired of plain single-colour sheets made from painted paper tissue. What I started doing instead was to source a textile pattern on the Internet, and scale it down. It could then be printed on paper and simply cut and folded it into the correct shape. This works well for tartan or any complex patterns that are typical but hard to paint. It is quick, easy, cheap and efficient.

A special feature sometimes available in Europe is a scale representation of the typical Danish plush. This material, typically red or

1. The latest plastic kits come with nicely detailed dashboard panels. The challenge is to paint them realistically.

2. Painted dashboards from CTM are available for most kits to speed up the process and make the modeller's life easier.

3. Most of the dashboards consist of two layers. Glazing the gauges can be done with white glue.

4. Once dry, the clear white glue adds depth to the gauges. No other painting is required.

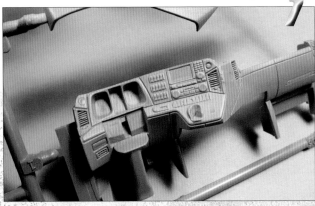

Woodgrain panels are typical for classic American trucks.

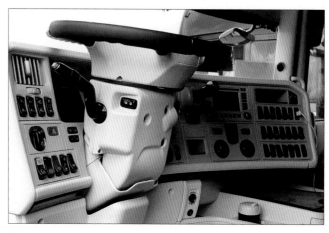

Modern custom trucks often have all the interior parts painted to the owner's liking.

blue, is used on modern custom trucks based on the traditional Danish style. It has a distinctive look and the self-adhesive imitation works well on flat surfaces. Apart from this, some generic fabric patterns are available from different decal producers and can be applied over seats, bunks or virtually any padded surface. In fact, if you can have your decals made for a specific pattern you can apply this on the upholstery too.

Many American trucks, as well as customised European examples, have specific leather upholstery. This is usually difficult to replicate as the padded structure is quite complex. However, some aftermarket companies offer the typical patterns in either soft styrene or resin sheets, which can be cut into pieces, painted and applied where needed.

If the aftermarket patterned sheets do not match your choice, there are other ways to go, however it needs real modelling or even sculpting skills. You can use one of the traditional modelling putties such as Miliput (Superfine White) or Magic Sculp, apply it over the part surface and get what you need using your skill and the appropriate tools. I have used this on a Scania engine tunnel in the cab, creating the classic padded upholstery that needed a Scania logo, which I created by pressing a photo-etched part into the surface before it had hardened.

5.4 DASHBOARDS

A dashboard is also virtually a model within a model. It is assembled separately, consists of many parts (especially if pedals are not located on the floor) and provides numerous detailing possibilities.

The finest of all dashboard details are always the control panels that comprise different gauges, buttons and displays. This is also true for other electronic equipment in the cab

or sleeper, such as CB radios or any control panels for heating, air conditioning or internal lights. In kits, the control panels are presented in two different ways. The older (AMT or Revell) offerings come with a relief of gauges and controls moulded to the kit parts. These are to be painted and that is quite demanding due to very fine detail. Hand painting needs both good paint and practice, but when balanced the results can be convincing and generally very good. As always, a fine brush and quality paints are necessary for that. A common way to make gauges or displays more authentic is to apply a drop of a gloss varnish over them to imitate glazing. The more varnish layers the better.

While brush painting dashboards has been the traditional method for many years, there are more advanced technologies. The CTM

photo-etched and painted dashboards appeared a few years ago, and offer both different buttons and switches, and a painted surface, resulting in very accurate parts that do not require additional painting – and are intended to replace the kit parts without modification.

Different details around the cab can be enhanced in a similar way. There are CB and AM/FM radios, modern tachographs as well as different heating or window control panels all over truck interiors. Some are available in the kits and only require hand painting. Many also feature in different CMT photo-etched sets.

A typical element seen on older trucks is wooden decor on the dashboard panels. You can either hand paint the wood using one of the methods used by WWI aircraft modellers,

A typical way of painting different signal lights and switches is to use different clear paints. These are best applied over a coat of white.

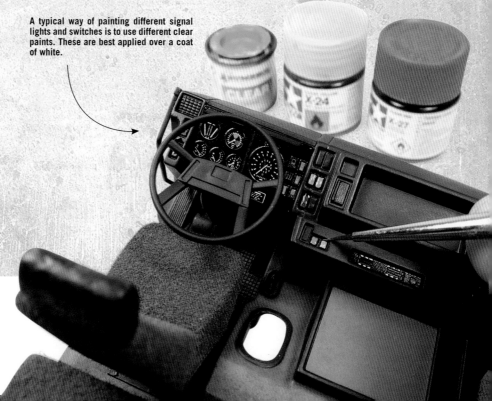

A factory version of the Scania 143 interior. Note the CB radio cable and the wrinkles on the seat.

> *Seatbelts are missing on most kit seats.*

which mostly involves using oil or enamel paints applied with a brush or sponge. Or you can use decals that are made as generic sheets for the same purpose, and reproducing wooden surfaces in general (HGW, Uschi van der Rosten, etc). These come in different versions and tones and can also be altered with the colour of the basic surface, allowing a wide range of effects.

The steering wheel is a distinctive part of any interior. Make sure the mould line all around the part is removed before painting and consider the real material of which the steering wheel is made. The classic large old wheels were glossy, usually black or white, while the plastic or leather versions are rather matt and need an appropriate finish. The steering column should be detailed with all the related controls for lights, wipers, trailer brake

or retarder, which are often missing in the kits but provide welcomed enhancement of the interior, especially when the driver's door is open. The same goes for pedals. These are either hinged in the dashboard or placed on the floor. In some kits, pedals may be missing or just simplified, but are usually included in various PE details sets.

Finally, we have the gear stick. While modern trucks are often equipped with automated transmission, classic vehicles mostly have a gear stick near the driver's seat. This also has details that may be added, particularly with more advanced vehicles with range and splitter transmissions, whereby the control switches are placed on the top of the stick. In cabover trucks the whole gear stick linkage needs attention, as not all trucks have the stick fitted to the cab floor, but instead it

is mounted via a support to the engine and remains there when the cab is tilted. Often the complete linkage to the transmission is missing, as are the air or cable lines operating the range and splitter functions.

Seatbelts can be made from a piece of plastic insulation tape, and the buckles are available in many PE sets.

1. All the interior upholstery in this Scania 141 interior was made from Tamiya putty, painted with acrylis and then treated with oil paint filters and washes.

2. Fine paper tissue is a good alternative, especially for old damaged seats.

1. Special made curtains are typical for European custom trucks.

2. Window curtains are included in most of European trucks to provide a bit of privacy for the driver. They are usually located behind the door window.

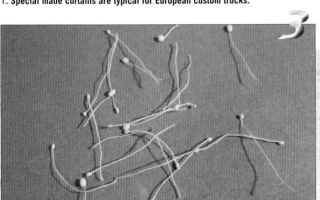

3. The bells for this custom made curtain were made of fine white thread and Miliput superfine white putty.

4. The individual bells were glued to the curtain.

5. The side curtains placed in the interior. Note the lamps on the rear wall, made in the same way as the curtains.

5.5 SEATS AND SEATBELTS

Techniques for seats basically follow what has been written on cab upholstery in general. Virtually all methods mentioned beforehand can be used for seat upholstery. The seats come in plastic while the real seats are soft and made of textile or leather, and the task is to make plastic look soft and have an accurate surface structure. It is also worth noticing the basic shape of the seats, as some kits provide incorrect parts and would benefit from resin upgrades.

The seatbelts usually are missing on most kit seats. There is a wide array of aftermarket parts to remedy this and they usually contain PE buckles, a piece of textile or vinyl strap and a seatbelt lock that is fitted to the seat. If not included in the set, the belt itself can always be made from a piece of black insulation tape cut to the correct width and length.

More details can usually be added around the seat suspension and controls. These are often simplified and the seat adjusting knobs are often missing – but can be improved with the help of styrene sheet, strip and rod. If the seat features air-suspension it usually has an external air inlet in the form of a thin black vinyl hose.

5.6 CAB ACCESSORIES

What brings the cab interiors to life more than anything else is everyday junk. It is basically everything the driver adds to the interior or needs in his 'office'. What I usually start with are magazines, newspapers, road maps, books or generic cargo documents. These can be found on the internet, scaled down in Microsoft Office Word and printed on a normal office printer. I like to place these around the interior and my favourite spot is the dashboard, where all these can be clearly visible on the finished model. Posters or calendars can be fashioned in a similar way and it's quick, cheap and very effective. Some scanning, graphics work and paper modelling may provide other subjects such as cigarette packs and any similar boxes, from food to spare parts. A cigarette pack in 1/24 is big enough to be displayed open with cigarettes in it. A cigarette can easily be made from a piece of thin Evergreen rod or a wire and placed in an ashtray if your model has one. A typical item that can easily be scratch built is a coffee mug which, again, can be placed anywhere in the driver's workplace. I like to use thin aluminium tube from K&S for the mug body, and a piece of wire for the handle.

If you want to expedite the detailing process there are aftermarket sets that may make life easier. There is a 1/35 scale bottle set from PlusModel, which offers items cast in both green and white clear resin and come with label decals. Their size is OK for 1/24 half-litre bottles and they look just great. Eduard makes an excellent set of painted photo-etched mobile phones, which are a beautiful addition to

> *A coffee mug is a typical thing that can be easily scratch-built and placed anywhere around the driver's seat.*

a modern interior and far better than anything one could sculpt and paint. KFS offers a comprehensive set with cab 'junk' that contains just about anything from a driver in a sleeping bag to a pan with fried eggs; this gives the modeller plenty of detail for any interior. Other embellishments can be sourced from most 1/24 Italeri accessories sets, providing

tools and various subjects commonly seen and used around cars and trucks: a bucket, a lifting jack, different tools or hats. Fujimi produces a useful set with all kinds of garage tools. There are many areas where similar parts can be found and those who keep their eyes open are usually able to get the most interesting and original items.

5.7 WINDOWS AND CLEAR PARTS

Cab glazing is not necessarily a part of the interior but forms the transition between the inside and outside of the cab... and it needs special attention as it can otherwise ruin all the work spent on the innards. The rules are basic and simple, yet many modellers still struggle with keeping their model windows clean and shiny. The first rule is to touch the clear parts as little as possible, or you will need to remove any grease or fingerprints from the clear parts, and you are then more likely to scratch or break them. Keep the clear parts sealed in the bag for as long as possible during the build and take them out just prior to the moment you need them.

The second rule is to not use any aggressive adhesives. Yes, the real masters may use Super Glue or standard modelling glue on

1. All sorts of interior details can be scratch-built. The sausage was made from a piece of sprue, and the bread from a kitchen sponge.

2. The CB radio panel comes from the pre-painted CTM interior PE set.

3. The shoes are resin items from KFS.

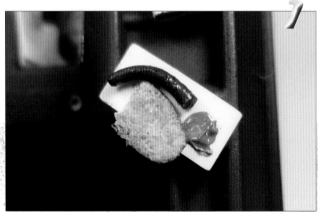

4. Some accessories, such as the Coke bottle in the picture, can be sourced from 1/35 scale accessories sets. All the maps and magazines were printed on a paper and cut out.

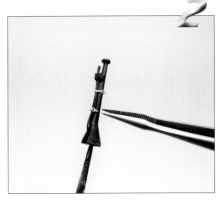

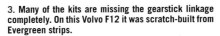

1. The pedals should not be missing in any model interior. These are etched items from the dedicated CTM set for Peterbilt trucks.

2. Some gearsticks have external air lines. The one in the picture is secured with etched cable ties.

3. Many of the kits are missing the gearstick linkage completely. On this Volvo F12 it was scratch-built from Evergreen strips.

clear parts, but this requires absolute control of what you are doing and there is no 'undo button'. I rather recommend using epoxy or white glue, which is less likely to damage the clear part. For smaller components, such as lights, a hint of varnish may be enough to fix the part in position.

If the clear part has been damaged with glue, paint or just simply scratched, repairs are still possible. Although very brittle, clear parts can be sanded and polished just like the final layer of paint. Starting with very fine abrasive paper (1,500 – 2,000) or sanding sticks, any surface damage (except for cracks of course) can be repaired. However, it needs time and patience. Cracks are harder to repair and, in most cases, a new windscreen has to be made from clear styrene sheet.

Rubber sealing around the glazing is also an obvious part of the window and visible on most trucks, so it should also be reproduced on a model. Just make sure to study actual photos of the real vehicle before you start. The rubber sealing can be carefully brush painted or sprayed after masking, and it's one of those details that may seem negligible – but in fact brings the model to life in the end. ■

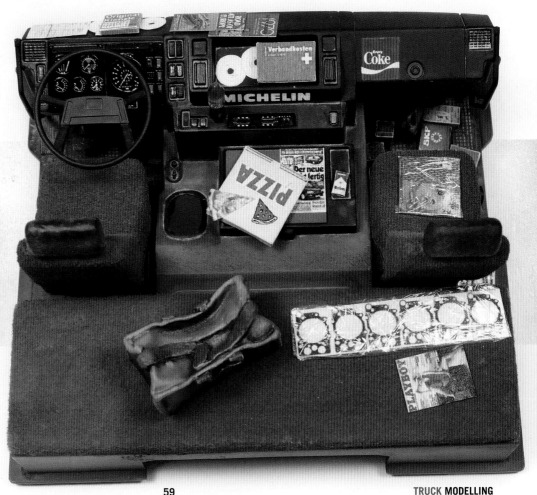

4. Truck interiors can be pretty busy. The bag on the bunk is a resin CTM item, and most of the remaining accessories were made from paper. Note the flocking used on the bunk and seats.

6 TRAILER KITS & T

Although I consider trailers to be just as important and interesting as trucks, they simply did not find their way into the previous book due to lack of space. So, let's go through the trailer kit offerings briefly before we will deal with building them.

6.1 TRAILER KITS

While trailer kits have appeared on the market together with trucks themselves, the number is relatively small. All renderings of the former come either from AMT/Ertl, Italeri or Revell. While AMT/Ertl stays within 1/25 to cater for its trucks, Italeri does the same with 1/24 trailers – and Revell offers both, from its own designs and those of Italeri. Recently, Moebius models has introduced two beautiful modern US Great Dane reefer trailers, and hopefully a modern

all- aluminium flatbed is coming soon. Heller produced a pair of decent 1/24 three-axle Trailor trailers (a canvas and a reefer), which are also good and repeatedly reissued. In addition, some aftermarket companies provide limited-edition trailer kits.These are mostly based on resin castings and CNC milled parts/3D printing and are arguably worthy alternatives. To name just some, Auslowe Model Accessories has a relatively wide choice of typically Australian trailers, and Dutch Model Truck Club is behind a small range of specific trailers including silo tankers.

A good thing about trailer kits in general is that they are mostly good. The AMT/Ertl items are pleasing and, despite their age, represent the real thing well enough and nicely match the available range of periodic tractors. There are dry van and reefer trailers, low loader, dumper and tanker trailer kits available, as well as a unit for livestock, a logging trailer, a single-axle car transporter and a moving van trailer. A classic flatbed has also been tooled, and so has a pair of single-axle trailers with a dolly. Yes, all these kits come from the 1970s, but many are

RAILER REFERENCES

still available due to repeated reissues. Furthermore, the quality is reasonable and most can be built straight from the box; just minor modifications can turn them into attractive models.

Revell made a few trailers from which a car transporter trailer and a Beall tank trailer are worth mentioning, together with some Michigan-type multi-axle trailers (a tanker, a flatbed and a gravel trailer). For European trucks (although the kit is in 1/25 scale) Revell made a heavy-duty low loader (No.7542). A special kit is the 1/24 Hanomag trailer made to fit the 50s Büssing and Krupp trucks and was well detailed. Just like AMT, Revell also re-issues its kits repeatedly and most are still available.

Except for one (American 48ft reefer trailer, No. 742 and following re-issues) all Italeri trailers represent European vehicles. It all started with a two-axle Fruehauf container trailer with a 40ft container (No. 754) in 1981, followed by an Italian-style three-axle tanker in 1982 (No. 758, later followed by No. 713, 3886, 3911). Other trailers were based on the tanker chassis: the canvas (No. 754), the container (No.3865) and frigo trailer (No. 791) of which all are pretty poor as the chassis and body combination do not represent anything realistic; it's typically Italian, with weird axle positions and fictional bodies. A canvas trailer (No. 774), a platform semitrailer (No.769) and a reefer trailer (No.3896) were made on the chassis

of the container trailer (No.742) and these are pretty fine, although the way the body sits on the chassis is not ideal. The Jumbo tank trailer (No. 725) looks cool (although the axles and suspension again come from the original tanker No. 758) and was also offered as a streamlined Topas version (No.73, as well as No. 3731). In 2001 Italeri introduced a brand-new curtainside trailer (No. 3809, and later decal versions 3918), which represents a good 13.6m Schmitz trailer – the most common type/make on European roads. This was later followed by a reefer (No.3813, 3904) and cargo trailer (No. 3835, 3885), both of which are worthy product. However, the reefer from this era should already be a unibody type. A beautiful addition to the 1/24

1-2. Revell Germany's contribution to the topic are the American trailer kits from the 90s. Tied to the name of their creator - Klaus Lassen - they represent a dream of one man that came true and who gave us modellers a chance to build authentic replicas.

3-5. Most of the modern European trailers offered by both the Revell and Italeri are based on the Schmitz curtainside trailer.

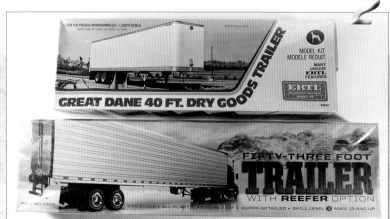

5. A limited series of special trailers was introduced by Dutch Model Truck Club. Apart from this bottom dump they also made a silo tanker, a 20ft container chassis and a cement mixer trailer.

1. Single axle dry vans have been used in both the double or triple combinations in the United states. The double combination including the dolly can be found in this AMT kit.

2. Comparing some of the kits reveals what has changed in the last fifty years. Both these kits represent the same type of trailer, just some fifty years apart.

3. The Fruehauf gravel trailer has been the only one dump trailer available until the Italeri Schmitz appeared relatively recently.

4. Back in the 70s AMT made a wide range of American trailers. Fifty years later, most of these kits are still available.

scale fleet is the Dumper trailer (No. 3845). A timber trailer (No. 3868) is also based on the Schmitz curtainsider, but has additional parts including the bumper, which allows the trailer to be constructed as a vehicle made by Austrian company Gsodam. The only trailer made by Italeri to be a real trailer (not a semi) was the Canvas trailer (No.766 and later No.3880), available either separately or in truck and trailer combinations with the Scania 142 or DAF 3300. The canvas body was used for both the truck and trailer and was included in all Italeri canvas trucks. The

same trailer chassis was also used with a drop-side body trailer in combination with a Scania 142 (No. 770). Most of the Italeri kits have been reissued with different decal versions and most are still available.

The most significant problem when building trailers is their size. Not only that the finished model occupies a lot of space in your display case, but all the filling and sanding is time consuming, especially when the trailer side and roof panels come in halves and need to be filled and sanded. The amount of paint you need for a trailer is also conside-

rably more and spraying a whole trailer with a 0.2 airbrush nozzle can be laborious. On the other hand, it is the trailer that gives your truck the correct proportions and its purposeful look, essentially completing the story.

6.2 TRAILER DESIGN

All that was said about brakes and suspension – and a good part of the air system on trucks in volume 1 of this book series – is valid for trailers. Either leaf spring suspension or air bags are commonly used on trailers all around the world. Hydraulics can be seen on

Trailer design

special applications such as heavy haulage trailers. The brakes are air operated and most of the trailers have only service brake chambers, and the parking brake is purely mechanical with a winch and hand- operated crank. Some trailers, however, are equipped with spring brake chambers that replace any other parking brake entirely. As for the brake type, in Europe disc brakes on trailers are standard nowadays, while the rest of the world still mostly soldiers on with drum brakes. The trailer axles, if not steerable, are mostly a simple tube with bearings on both ends, on which the wheel hubs spin. Steerable axles are common in some areas and for some applications, and the designs can vary with the trailer origin and age; from a simple trailer turntable and a rigid axle to a highly complex linkage system with a steering king pin, and operated either mechanically or via hydraulics.

Trailer frames and bodywork have many shapes and the architecture again differs with the country of the trailer origin. Obviously, the trailers are meant to be cheap, light and simple. The only thing we expect from them is to be attachable to a truck and carry a load. Basically, they represent just a pair of frame rails with cross members, to which axles and bodywork are attached… and that's it. Some trailers with a rigid body

structure (dry vans, reefer trailers or tankers) often have no frame at all. Still, there are different 'schools' and not all trailers are the same. The differences are not just caused by local tendencies and habits, but especially by length and weight restrictions. It may be an oversimplification, but in general one can say that there are three basic 'trailer architecture' streams displaying the typical features, and the rest of the world follows one of them while the basic idea is still the same. These three schools are the following: European, American (USA) and Australian. If you park a trailer from each of these next to each other, you will immediately be able to tell them apart and explain the differences. Of course, the further you go from general transport trailers to special purpose vehicles, more and more differences and individual traits may appear… but that is far beyond the scope of this article.

The US school keeps trailers simple and classic. Typical features are two axles with twin-mounted wheels (although you can now see super single wheels in the US regularly), often fitted as a sliding subframe assembly for changing the weight distribution, simple design and mostly with minimal add-ons; no tool boxes, no underrun bars, no palette boxes, no spare wheel carriers or mudgu-

ards and the like. However, what American trailers have, and others don't, is that many are constructed from aluminium and this has been so since the 1940s-50s – which is most likely related to war machinery and the amount of aluminium necessary for building World War Two aircraft. This most likely ensured a reasonable aluminium price in the post-war period. While simple overall, certain smart features are evident on US trailers. To name some, I would point out the way that cargo is secured on flatbeds, with sliding winches for ratchet straps, or the modern canvas flatbeds with sliding tarp systems.

The European school also used to have a fairly simple two axle semitrailer design, but the shapes and sizes varied across the different countries, and were standardised in the late 1960s-70s as the regulations became more common all over. Things were far from unified in comparison to today's world. The early 80s fostered replacing the classic two-axle trailers with dual wheels, with modern three-axle trailers and super single tyres, which is a model still used in Europe today except for the length, which has increased from 12.5m to 13.6m over the years. Twin-mounted wheels are becoming relatively rare and most modern equipment runs on super single wheels. Disc brakes on trailers appeared just after the year 2000, as well as modern electronics for brakes and vehicle stabilisation controls. While in detail the European trailers may seem smartly designed (loads of accessories, mudguards, tool boxes and spare wheel carriers, fancy brake systems, practical curtainsider systems) an average trailer still has a classic steel frame. Zinc plating became more popular instead of painting frames. Aluminium is commonly used for lightweight dump trailers and silo tankers, but only for both the frames and bodywork. If a dry van trailer is a common sight in the US, such a type of trailer has never been widely used across Europe; the most common variant of vehicle for general transport is a three-axle curtainsider trailer.

Australia is a good example of a place where both premium American and European equipment meets. Furthermore, 'down under' is where the heaviest truck and trailer combinations are operated, often in areas where gravel roads are common and the going can be very severe. Studying an average Australian semitrailer (possibly a three-axle curtainsider), one can tell that it is pretty close to what is used in Europe. The trailers often have mudguards and various toolboxes and water tanks, which gives them a European look. However, the twin-mounted wheels are still standard here, giving the trailers a more classic, old-school appearance, and both the spider or aluminium rims make them look more American. For the well-known road train combinations, the so-called 'dollies' are used to carry a fifth wheel and attach one trailer to another and apart from those, there are also different trailer types that carry a fifth wheel to form various B-train combinations that sometimes employ clever sliding body or axle solutions for loading/unloading. Just as in Europe, a common trailer chassis in Australia is also made of steel rather than aluminium, which is mostly employed for lightweight dump trailers.

There will always be exceptions in trailer design in some areas, prompted by abnormal weight limits and length restrictions used locally such as in the US (Michigan), Brazil, Canada or South Africa, Europe (Netherlands, Scandinavia) or Australia (different road train sizes allowed in different parts of the country), which always mean that trailers here appear different, but describing all of them is not the purpose of this chapter. I only wanted to highlight that in different parts of the world, trailers vary and have their specific features, so this should be considered when building models. ■

Tank trailers

1. Bulk silo tankers are usually welded from aluminium sheets and the American ones are often nicely polished. Note the amount of additional equipment.

2. Fuel tankers in Michigan are very specific for their higher bodies and a number of axles. Even on this modern example four of the main axles are running on leaf springs.

3. Typical American tankers are long and slim. Often made of aluminium they can be both polished to a high shine, or dull and weathered. A Beall trailer kit from Revell represents this type.

4. A short 20ft container trailer with a tank container is the latest trailer kit made by Italeri. Note at the intense weathering on the tank walls.

5. This early 90s Trailor tanker had its life extended many times. It still looks fresh with the latest tractors which means that by changing the wheels, mudguards and a bumper even the Italeri kits may be upgraded effectively.

6. This is a typical modern European fuel tanker. The body can be sourced from the Italeri Topas tanker but it would need an air suspension from the Schmitz kit for example.

7. Tipping silo is another type commonly used in Europe. With all the details they represent an attractive model and even a limited resin kit was available recently.

8. Various lockers and boxes for different valves, pumps and measuring instruments are all typical features of a tank trailer.

65

Canvas trailers

1. A Modern Michigan steel coil trailer. The gross weight limit of these combinations in Michigan is 164,000 pounds on 11 axles.

2. Another type of coil trailer but this one has drop sides and is running on super single wheels.

3. The rounded tail lights and marker lights combination and minimalistic design is typical for most American trailers.

4. Sliding tarp systems on flatbed trailers are commonly seen on the roads in the United States as an alternative to classic open flatbeds.

5. European trucks in the 50s and 60s were commonly using leather belts to tighten up the canvas.

1. This truck and trailer combination is a European classic.

2. All kinds of tool boxes and water kegs were used on trailers on the Middle East runs back in the 70s and 80s.

3. A two axle spread axle tilt trailer in Astran livery. It cannot be more classic. This company were famous for their Middle East routs.

4. Horizontal TIR cord and a vertical belt, a standard closing system of a classic European canvas trailers.

5. Modern European trailers have evolved from two axle twin mounted wheels to three axle versions with super single tyres during the 80s. Note this Czechoslovakian BSS trailer has a steerable rear axle.

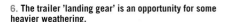

6. The trailer 'landing gear' is an opportunity for some heavier weathering.

7. The typical trailer length in Europe was changed from 12.5m to 13.6m during the 80s. The dropside canvas bodies were standard until the end of the century.

Dry van trailers

1. Moderm European reefer trailer bodies are mostly made from plastic.

2. Not really a dry van or reefer but a cattle 'pot', a common trailer type across the United States. Nowadays often made of stainless or aluminium.

3. A nice detail of the manual lock mechanism of the sliding undercarriage on a 70s Fruehauf dry van.

4. Scandinavia has different lengh, height and weight limits for trucks, so 25.25 metre 60 tonne combinations are typical there.

5. Aluminium trailers have been widely used in the United States since WWII.

1. Some modern American reefers still have the old look. The classic stainless version is still available and the spread axle versions are still popular.

2. A typical rear end of an European trailer. Schmitz is probably the most common brand across Europe.

3. Unlike the Italeri Schmitz reefer, the modern European trailers are "unibody" which means they have no full length frame anymore.

4. Long mudflaps with all sorts of anti-sail features are typical for American trailers.

5. The old 50s trailer were often streamlined with nicely curved front walls. Note how short whey were.

6. A pair of air hoses and an electric cables in the middle, all hanging from a pogo stick. A typical American setup.

7. Container trailers are popular all around the world. This is a European rigid non-extendable 40ft version.

Flatbed trailers

1. Step deck trailers are a common way to increase the volume capacity in the United States.

2. A classic all-aluminium flatbed semitrailer in a spread axle configuration. Note the additional toolbox between the axles.

3. Another typical rear end of an American trailer. Note it is all aluminium and stainless.

4. The sliding strap winches are a typical thing for American flatbeds that cannot be seen in Europe.

5. To keep within the weight limits given by the bridge formula, all sorts of extensions and additional axles can be seen on different trailers.

1. Note that this flatbed trailer hauling mining truck tires is a rather unusual type with axles close together and super single tires.

2. Flatbeds often carry all sorts of straps and winches needed for securing the cargo properly.

3. Ropes and sheets have been a traditional way of securing cargo in the United Kingdom.

4. Toolboxes are not very typical for American trailers but are often seen on flatbeds, holding chains and straps.

5. Oversize loads in the United States are moved with some relatively simple lowboy trailers.

6. A nice detail of the tarp and ropes used to secure the load of barrels on classis british lorry.

7. These lowboy trailers can create extremely long and complex combinations with added goosenecks and axle extensions.

7 SCHMITZ CURTA

It cannot be more classic or typical. Speaking of modern European trailers, three-axle 13.6m curtainsiders are what moves Europe. This type of trailer has replaced the classic drop-side canvas versions often previously used on the continent and have been a common sight on European highways since the mid-1990s.

NSIDE TRAILER

7.1 INTRODUCTION

While in the US the transportation of goods is split between dry vans and flatbeds, curtainsiders do it all in Europe and only specialised tasks are tackled by reefers. Dry vans are almost non- existent in Europe. A modern curtainsider is such a universal tool and Schmitz is the most common brand seen and employed everywhere.

Back in the late '90s the situation on the market with trailer kits was sad. The length laws extending the modern trailer length from 12.5 to 13.6m were valid for many years but

model builders had absolutely nothing to work with. All we had were the obsolete Italeri examples, of which the three-axle variant was never good. Based on a rather specific Italian design, Italeri pretended it could turn it into a generic modern trailer but it simply didn't work; the dimensions and proportions were weird. At least the Heller trailers were good but too old to resemble any modern 1990s equipment. Then, finally, in 2001 Italeri announced a modern three-axle curtainsider trailer from Schmitz and later its derivatives (a reefer and a drop-side tilt trailer) that have changed it all. Not only that, new air suspension and disc brakes came too. Converting the Schmitz into other makes, by changing the rear bumper and other details all around, has also been easy since then.

7.2 PLANNING

I have been thinking about building the curtainsider myself too. I liked the idea of using a Solartex on the curtains, and photo-etched buckles and straps to replace the simple plastic items. I bought the kit long ago and have collected all the necessary accessories over the years; however, the right impulse simply did not come… and it is quite easy to explain why. I usually start my builds with the tractor. I always have an idea of a trailer I would like to build for it but during construction of the tractor itself I am usually happy to finish just the truck, not speaking of the trailer. Then

I move to another truck, and another, and that is the way it's been for years. This trailer should have already been built for the Iveco Stralis you may know from my first book, but I never managed to start working on it. However, in gathering all the material for the upcoming publication, it was evident that trailers were one of the important topics that did not find its way into the first book - and that a modern European trailer was vital.

As I'd been planning the build of this trailer for a while I had most of the necessary accessories and quite a good idea what it should look like. My timing was tight but that was one of the reasons why I decided to go for the curtainsider. It can be efficiently detailed with pleasing little nuances all around, and for those who want to go further there is the conversion to Solartex canvas, and photo-etched buckles and straps available. I did not want to get carried away too much with converting a kit that is actually very good and accurate from the start, but I also had a list of things I wanted to try on the model. In the end the list of accessories turned out to be pretty long and the price of the extras was about four times that of the original kit (so, yes, I got carried away a little…) but it was all in the name of successfully finishing the trailer on time. I liked the Solartex, but I also knew that if it was employed all around, I could avoid painting the large body areas and be less dependent on filling the halves between the trailers. I liked the

Kit: Revell 07562 Schmitz curtainside trailer
Scale: 1/24
Accessories: MCA aluminium wheels, Solartex curtains, CTM 24046 Curtainsides straps and buckles, CTM 24096 Hamburger lights, KFS decals, CTM 24199 Modern European marker lights, CTM 24076 ADR Petrol and diesel tanker boards, KFS Air valves, DMTC 24-500 light housings
Notes: A kit manufactured by Italeri, boxed with different decals by Italeri and Revell

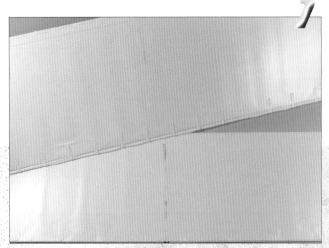

1. Filling and sanding is usually required as most trailer walls come in halves rather than full lenght.

2. Using a wet sanding paper and water speed up the process and provided a smoother results.

3. The parts´ fit was far from perfect so the upper body edges were roughly adjusted with the scalpel prior to the filling.

4. Instead of applying the Tamiya putty directly from the tube, I thinned it with acetone and applied it with a flat brush.

> *When it comes to trailers, the main thing that makes building them different is their size.*

photo-etched buckles and straps and knew that even sticking with the originals moulded on the trailer sides, it would all take too long to paint convincingly. I have always wanted to try some of the MCA aluminium rims with real nuts and bolts and I knew they would look superb and save time on painting the rims accurately. While the original square tail lights were perfectly acceptable, and I knew I could use clear replacements from Italeri's accessories set no.720, but it was also obvious that if I used the CTM photo-etched hamburger lights I would again save painting time.

When it comes to trailers the main thing that makes building them different is their size. This one is almost 570mm long and that means much cleaning of parts, filling and painting. The Italeri trailers have all the body panels split into halves, so they need precise filling and sanding, otherwise it will ruin the overall appearance. I have never accepted rough filling and sanding, but ultimately it was not so bad on this model. I have used Tamiya's classic putty, and after the initial sanding and priming the result was quite good. The original straps and buckles were removed with a hand-held Proxxon mill. The surface would need some refinement had it all been just painted, but as I knew that the Solartex goes over that, I was ok with what I had.

7.3 SOLARTEX SURFACE

Solartex has been used on curtainsider trailers for many years and it is one of the basic updates that can enhance Italeri's kit. As for

my trailer colour scheme, I knew I wanted to build something universal for any of my existing European tractor builds – or any I would complete in the future – rather than anything specific. So I opted for a white roof and blue sides, one of the most common European configurations. I hadn't worked with Solartex before but a friend of mine, Ashley Coghill, has and he was willing to share his experience with me before I started. As I wanted to save as much time as possible, I decided to apply the material not just on the sides but on the roof as well. I therefore started with a white roof. I cut a sheet slightly oversized in length and about 30mm extra in width, before fixing the side edge along the upper side edge on one side of the trailer. It was then stretched over the roof to the other side wall and fixed there. This was done with superglue and the whole top panel was left unglued, with just a few localised creases. The sides were attached with white glue, which was applied

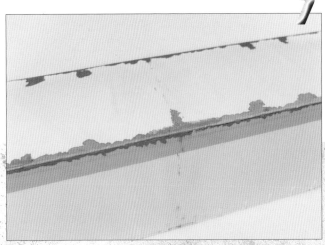

1. As mentioned in the text, the trailer bodies were large and required lots of filling and sanding.

2. A Proxxon Mill helped removing the original plastic buckles.

3. Using a Mr.Surfacer spray can was a lot quicker than using an airbrush on these large surfaces.

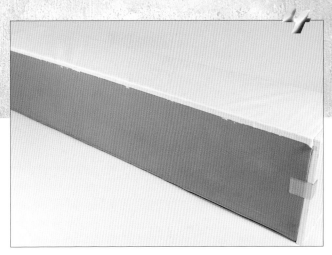

4. Solartex on the roof was applied first with super glue, only along the edges.

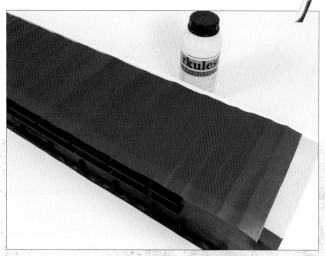

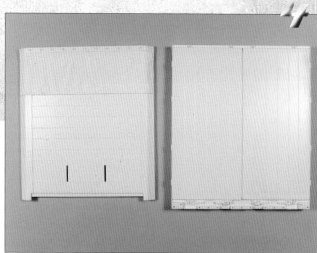

To make the aluminum parts of the trailer a bit more interesting I used Tamiya X-19 Smoke over the basic Gunze silver No.8 for shading.

1. I creased the Solartex a little bit before it was applied on the side wall.

2. I used a white water based glue and applied it underneath the canvas.

3. As the glue was drying I smoothened the side to my liking and pushed out all the unwanted air bubbles.

4. Both the front and rear walls were beautifully detailed. I only added the Solartex for the front.

5. The real side walls are zinc plated steel so I used Alclad steel as a base and then Gunze silver for the sponge method.

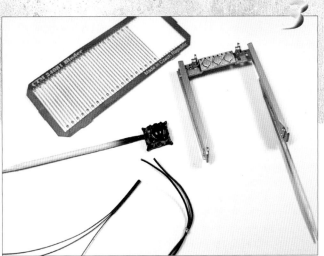

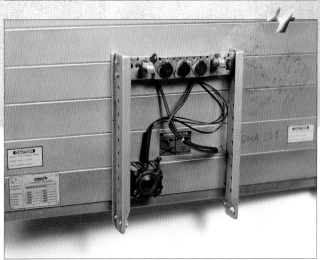

1. A wide choice of decals always helps when searching for some good authentic ones. These are mostly KFS decals that are no longer available unfortunately.

2. Rubber bump stops on the rear the were hand painted. Most of the decals come from CTM, and specifically, the speed limits were taken from the CTM Berliet kit.

3. The suzie bracket in the kit was nicely detailed and just needed a few air lines and a fuse box from KFS.

4. The difference betwen the Italeri and Revell kits are often in the small details. While Italeri has nothing, the Revell decals include both the silver and blue data plates, both beautiful.

Note the sticky surface remaining from the removed ADR stickers. Those are for sea transport purposes only and are to be removed before the truck goes back on the road again.

on the whole side panel as I wanted a solid base for the etched buckles in later steps. The bottom creases were just a copied surface of the original plastic, but here the canvas was fixed with superglue to ensure the creases were copied properly. With the bottom sprayed in dark grey using a spray can, before the canvas was applied, there were just the front and rear walls missing and the basic body was finished. Test fitting revealed the fit of these panels was nearly perfect, so I could easily finish them separately and add them to the canvas-covered body without risk.

7.4 PAINTING

The rear door, as well as the front wall, are made of extruded aluminium panels and just the front corner reinforcements are steel, often zinc-plated. I wanted to add realism and did not just want to spray both ends silver, leaving them flat and dull. I used a Mr.Color silver No.8 applied over Mr.Finishing Surfacer Black as a base coat. Then I covered some of the panels with Tamiya masking tape and sprayed thinned Tamiya X-19 Smoke, making some panels darker and more stained. I continued with darker Alclad metallic tones such as Steel and Jet Exhaust, and then masked the front corners and sprayed them with Steel completely. As they are zinc-plated I used a piece of kitchen sponge to apply irregular dots of different metallic colours, emulating real chips. It all went well and within an hour of adding black primer I was already applying decals to both the front wall and rear door. I used a mixture of decals, mostly made by KFS (data plates, trailer manufacturers and some older discontinued sets), some from the original Revell kit and others from my various kit leftovers. All I was using were generic data plates, signs and stickers employed across Europe and I mostly took inspiration from various rental trailers. The hazard stickers (from CTM's Hazmat set) were placed according to the IMDG Code used for trailers shipped on

1. The front and rear walls fit perfectly. I had no issues even with the Solartex.

2. The kit frame was rather basic and building it was relatively quick.

3. It was vital to keep everything perfectly square.

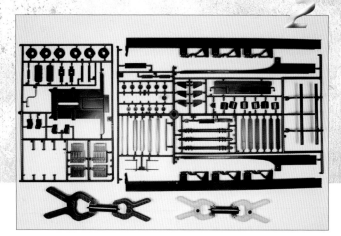

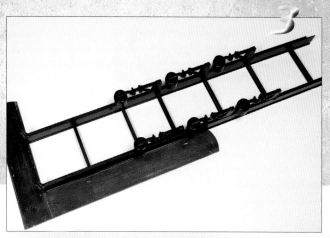

4. The kit frame rails came in halves. To get the fit perfectly straight, I used a pair of clips to secure the parts together.

5. The frame was primed with Mr.Surfacer, applied with an airbrush.

1. The Italeri set for detailing trailers contains nicely detailed mudguards but the mounts need some rework and test fitting and the suggested combination does not work on the Schmitz.

2. A correct combination of mounts was required to do the job. Those that fitted the Schmitz were actually used for much older trailers.

3. Easy and effective, the mudguars helped improving the kit a lot.

4. I wanted to show some typical pallet box wear so I employed the hair spray technique and used a ruler to make the scratches straight.

5. Oils and pigments were used for the weathering. Nothing too complex, it was a quick job.

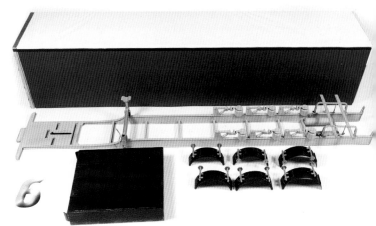

6. The separate assemblies prior to the final frame painting.

vessels; it is not absolutely correct but I found it on some old trailers for sale and did it like that. The orange ADR and reflective boards are CTM items, and so are the French-style speed limit plates. The removed sticker traces were painted with acrylics and oils, while the susie bracket came straight from the kit. I only added a pair of my own resin air couplings. The electric box was a KFS part and the wiring made from black nylon fishing line.

7.5 FRAME AND CHASSIS

The next step was the frame. Again, just like the side walls, the frame rails usually come in halves or multiple pieces and all the joinsmust be filled and sanded. To minimise the gaps and secure a correct geometry of the rails and crossmembers, I always use a metal square and generic clamps to hold together the parts while the glue hardens. That way, just one round of filling and sanding was needed on the frame rails, as well as on the palette box. The suspension is moulded on the rails and just some airbag halves need to be added. These needed filling/sanding, but as most of it would be covered with wheels and hidden under the body I carried out just the basic operations and left the rest straight from the kit. The

landing gear comes straight from the kit as well and so does the spare wheel carrier and fire extinguisher box. The small toolbox on the right-hand side of the trailer was from Italeri's accessories set No.720. The rear bumper was modified with CTM hamburger light lenses fitted on 3D-printed light housings No. 24-500, offered by Dutch Model Truck Club. All the reflectors, both the rounded and triangular versions, came from the CTM 24098 trailer reflectors set. Wiring for the lights was made from black fishing nylon and a KFS wire junction box.

The pallet box is a typical item that gets scratched and beaten on many trailers. I wanted to show some signs of that on my trailer too. I therefore painted the sides silver and applied two layers of TresTwo hairspray. Once dry, I sprayed over it with Mr.Finishing Surfacer Black. Then I used a hard brush for wearing the edges, but for replicating straight and

thin scratches I used a scalpel to cut through the black paint first. This let the water get to the hairspray underneath and, with just a little time and gentle brush work along the cut, a pleasing straight scratch can be made easily. The rest of the effects were created with oil paints and pigments.

To make the trailer look a little different I used individual mudguards instead of the kit's quarter fenders. The mudguards and mounts came from the Italeri accessories set No.3870

and needed slight mount modifications, but look the part.

What has always been a big topic for me are the wheels. I like good looking tyres and rims, and I wanted some on my trailer. Luckily, the Italeri trailer super single tyres looked perfect, so there was no need to replace them, but the standard rims were outdated and more of a late 1980s / early 90s design. The previously mentioned set with mudguards contains the latest Italeri trailer rims, which are not bad…

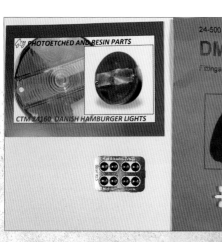

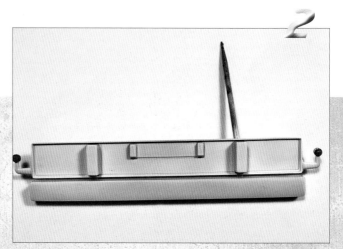

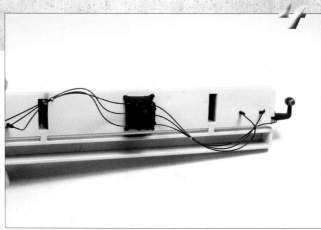

1. 3D printed light housings from my friends in the Netherlands were used for the CTM lights.

2. The bumper itself was a nice and authentic part. I only removed the original lights and replaced them with the typical "hamburgers" later on.

3. Both the tail lights and reflectors are photo etched CTM items. The rubber blocks were handpainted with Vallejo acrylics.

4. An additional fuse box and black vinyl line were used for the wiring.

5. The fire extenguisher box came with the kit and just the glazing made of a clear office tape was added.

1. Real aluminium wheels were used.

2. Assembly with bolts took more time than one may think but in the end they look perfect, although the bolts may be slighty oversized.

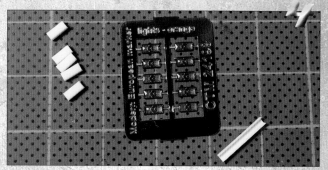

3. Heavily modified wheel hubs were used on the standard axles.

4. PE lights were adopted for marker lights all around the trailer.

but not great either. I especially do not like the hole shapes, which is unfortunately caused by the draft directions and moulding technology. What I wanted the trailer to look like it was from the 90s or early 2000s so it would fit behind anything from the late F12 to MP4 Actros. I therefore did not need anything modern, and finally decided to use MCA real aluminium deep dish wheels. These come with generic hubs, only I wanted some 90s-looking hubs so I simply cut out the hubs from the old

Italeri wheels and modified them to suit MCA's wheels, which are not that deep. The centre nuts came from an old Italeri trailer kit and the hub details are photo-etched parts I got from a friend, Gergö Kustánczi. These hubs were attached to the axles that did not need any modifications and came straight from the box. Each of the MCA wheels has 10 separate bolts and nuts. The latter are slightly oversized for 1/24 scale and assembly takes time and patience, but I must admit that tackling this

is really a unique experience, with a fantastic result that is worth the monetary outlay.

Since the early planning stages I knew that one of the keystones of this build would be making the CTM photo-etched straps and buckles, and that it would take a decent amount of time. Well, it did - and it took about 25 hours to bend and assemble all 44 straps and buckles used on the trailer, but I built a few more as the CTM sets contain excess parts in case of any butter-fingered accidents.

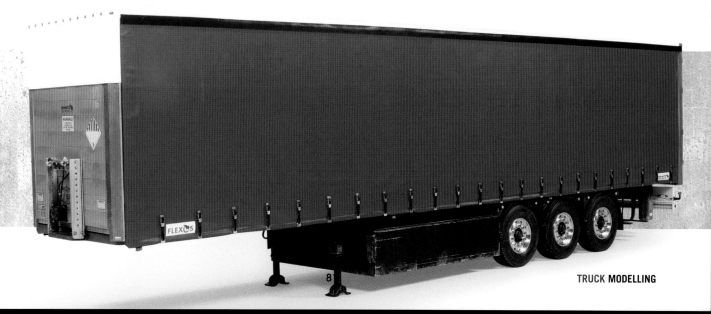

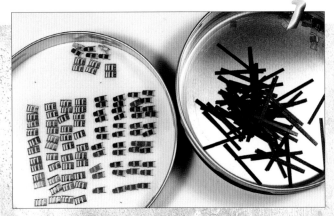

1. Assembling the curtainsider straps and buckles took time - a minimum of 44 sets had to be assembled.

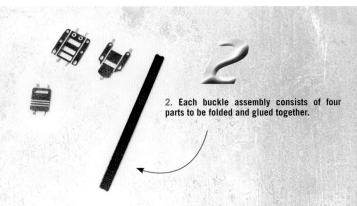

2. Each buckle assembly consists of four parts to be folded and glued together.

3. The strap has to be bent slowly and carefully to prevent the paint from peeling.

4. All the parts together ready for assembly accumulated about 25 hours of work.

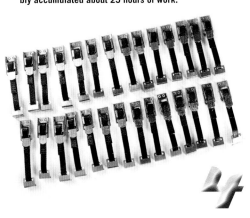

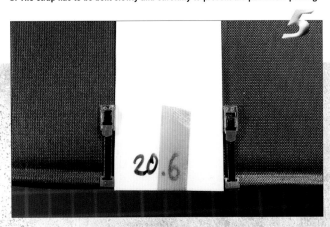

5. I made a stencil to keep the distance between the parts roughly the same.

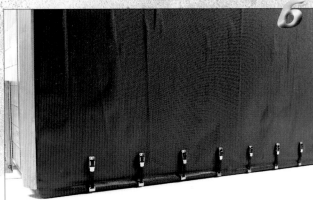

6. It was the combination of Solartex and PE details that brought the model to life.

The process for bending and assembling one, set is easy – but the laborious part is to repeat everything precisely 50 times. When finished, however, the results are much finer and more authentic than that offered by the original kit. According to the box art there are 22 buckles on each side. Using elementary maths, I found out I needed an approximate 20mm gap in between them. I made a stencil out of plastic and used that to determine the spaces one after another. The buckles were fixed with superglue and unlike their assembly the installation was easy and straightforward.

Once the buckles were added the body was married to the frame using both Tamiya Extra Thin and an epoxy glue for extra strength. The last components to be added were the marker lights that, again, came from the CTM set… both the clear versions on the front and the orange equivalents along the trailer sides. Wheel hubs and tyres were treaded with fine oil paint wash, but the rims and canvas were left untouched as that's what a universal trailer should look like.

SUMMARY

Once again, as with the case of the AMT dry van, I avoided building a trailer such as this for years, but once it was finished, I can only say it was not so bad. With good planning, smart accessories and just a little over two weeks I was able to finish something I had dreamed of for a very long time. ■

No specific tractor was ready for the trailer. However, the lack of signwriting and the very universal combination of parts and accessories make it universal for any truck from mid 90s to 2010.

8 PETERBILT 350 8

In terms of complexity trailers are often easier to build than trucks as there is no complex engine, no interior or other details. The challenge is, however, in their size which can make the assembly, filling, sanding and painting demanding.

FRUEHAUF DRY VAN

8.1 INTRODUCTION

The fact that I haven't built a trailer in the last decade was a bit daunting for me as everyone around me was successfully finishing them from time to time. The right moment came a few years back when I was planning a combination of a 50s-style US 'drom box' (signifying 'dromedary') tractor and an AMT dry van. The tractor originally should have been a GMC Cannonball and the trailer was meant to be mostly out of the box, but I failed to complete it for various reasons. Later I decided to split the GMC cab and the trailer and build

them separately. I took the GMC frame, which was generic enough, test-fitted a Peterbilt 350 COE cab on it and at that moment this project was born.

8.2 THE DRY VAN

The trailer was meant to be constructed out of the box, as the kit was decent enough and only needed small modifications or add-ons. What I like about it (despite its 50-year vintage) is the detailed side walls integrally moulded ribs and rivets. The trailer walls come in one piece for the whole trailer length, which significantly reduces the build effort

and need for filling. The box assembly went well except for the rear door, which did not fit very well. Additional Evergreen strips and profiles were required here to fill the gaps and tidy the area. The seam along the roof edge needed just minor sanding and filling. As the trailer is the unibody type there is no actual frame at all, apart from a pair of short frame rails on which the axle assembly can slide, to maintain the correct axle loads for both the truck and trailer – a typical feature on American trailers for decades. The axle assembly consists of a short ladder frame, leaf spring suspension and axles. This area is

TECH SPEC Peterbilt 350

Kit: AMT Fruehauf dry van trailer, resin cab from Pavel Behensky (limited run)
Scale: 1:25
Accessories: CTM 24092 US tail lights, CTM 24118 US trailer reflectors, my own resin wheels, Page and Page resin suspension, CTM etched head lights
Notes: Decals drawn by Jan Mostek and printed by decalprint.de

represented well and I did not add anything here except for brake lines. Even the thin 'anti-sail' mud flaps are realistic enough, so I used them straight from the box. What I did not like were the rough and poorly detailed wheels, so I used my own resin wheels and tyres I made for another project, which happened to fit perfectly. The trailer support legs come as a separate assembly too, and I built this as per the instructions without any need for additional detailing. All the lights on the model were replaced with CTM photo-etched items. The trailer taillights come from CTM's 24092 Taillights set and the side reflectors

and marker lights from CTM 240118 Truck and trailer reflectors.

While the side walls were painted aluminium, I used light grey for the trailer door and medium grey for the roof and lower side walls. As the lower side walls and rear bumper are made of steel, these were primed with Mr.Finishing Surfacer Black, with a hint of brown added to it, over-sprayed with chipping fluid from AK Interactive and followed by Tamiya acrylic grey. Gentle hairspray technique chipping was also employed to create mild and subtle chipped paint effects.

Applying the decals was challenging be-

cause of the ribbed walls. I used custom-made decals (drawn by Jan Moštěk and printed by decalprint.de), and very carefully I cut out each of the large letters to get rid of any clear decal film, and applied them separately using both Mr.Mark Setter and Mr.Mark Softer decal agents. It was the most difficult part of the build and took two evenings. Once dry, the decals were sealed with a fine coat of Mr.Color Super Clear varnish.

The PE number plates come from the Peterbilt 350 kit, which I painted in two steps. It takes practice, but the results can be convincing. Once all the details were added, a dark

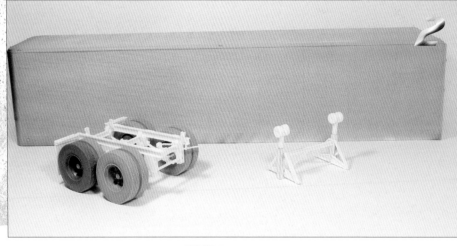

1. No modifications were required on the frame and all the parts except the wheels came straight from the kit.

2. All the main assemblies ready for painting. Note that there is no frame, unlike the Schmitz trailer in chapter 7. On this type of trailer it is the body that carries the whole weight.

3. Dark grey was used on the undercarriage before a quick weathering with oils. A light dust was applied all over the parts and then some stains and streaks were painted with oils and blended with thinner on tyres and mud flaps.

4. Most of the body structure on the real trailer was made of aluminum. To simulate this, I painted the body with multiple Alclad metallic paints. A black oil paint wash was used to highlight the ribbed structure and rivets.

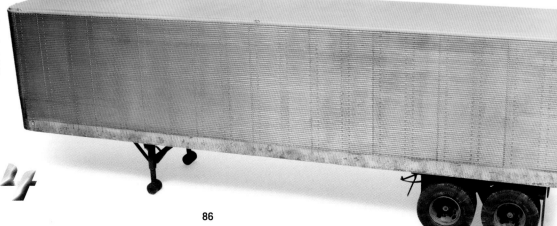

1. I made a several chipping attempts along the bottom edge of the trailer and many of them did not turn out the way I wanted.

2. Finally I masked the lower areas with Tamiya tape and sprayed it with a dark rust tone.

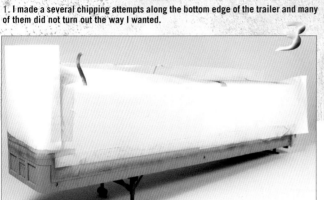

3. The dark rust was followed by a chipping fluid and then light grey Tamiya acrylic.

4. Once the surface was wet, I only used a sharp scalpel for creating the finest chips.

5. The custom made decals need to be cut into pieces first due to the covering clear film.

6. One by one, the letters were placed into the lukewarm water for a moment. With some decals the separation from the paper may take minutes. There is no need to rush this stage.

7. Placing the decals on the ribbed wall may be tricky. A drop of Mr.Mark Setter was applied underneath and than the decal was aligned perfecly with the horizontal ribs.

8. There is always some water and excess Setter underneath the decal. I use cotton buds to roll over the decal and pust it out and remove it.

9. Once placed properly with any bubbles of water from underneath removed, a fine coat of Mr.Mark Softer was applied over the decal.

10. A flat brush is suitable to ensure the decal copies all the surface details. Be careful as after the decal is very vulenrable once the softener is applied.

oil paint wash was applied over the trailer walls to highlight the ribbed structure. Brighter dust and dirt oil paints were used on the wheels and mud flaps, and all the hair spray chips were treated with rust colour tones.

8.3 PETERBILT 350 COE (1/25, RESIN CONVERSION)

Once the trailer was finished, I turned my attention to the truck. What was left from the GMC was not the Peterbilt chassis and it was fine because it was generic enough. I love the American trucks from the 50s. For me that was the golden age of trucking where the vehicles were already big and powerful, performing long trips but still displaying antique features – many of which quickly disappeared in the 1960s. Count with me: the Bullnose and Bubblenose type cabovers (because of

the length laws), wide use of two-stroke diesel engines, petrol engines still used for heavy duty trucks, mechanical blowers used for supercharging engines, the use of main and auxiliary transmissions and multi-speed axles for more gear combinations, worm drive axles, extensive use of aluminium. The earliest vehicles did not even have indicator lights and used mechanical arms to show the direction. The first time I saw a vehicle from this period was in the British documentary Classic Trucks. Here, footage of a Peterbilt 350 cabover tractor in the Pacific Intermountain Express livery was shown, and I immediately fell in love with it. The footage comes (as I found later) from the 1950s movie Wheels of Progress presented by PIE (available on youtube).

However, building a truck from this period

is not easy. It means you need a resin cab if you do not fancy scratch-building your own, and you need patience as many of the parts for these models have to be converted from other kits or fashioned from scratch. Therefore, building such a vehicle remained only a dream of mine for more than a decade. A few years ago, I had the chance to lay my hands on one of the Bubblenose Peterbilt cabs made by Pavel Behenský. The cab is beautifully cast and comes with PE parts.

8.3.1 CHASSIS

The chassis was originally built for the GMC Cannonball. The model ended up unfinished in a box and it took me two years to realise I no longer liked the original model's concept. However, the chassis, suspension, axles and wheels were too good to be thrown away and

New wheels, custom made decals and just a little bit of weathering can help you to make the 40 year old kit different and attractive.

Initial idea.

1. This frame was originally built for the GMC, now in chapter 11 of this book.

2. CNC milled set made by KFS was used for the frame rails and crossmembers.

3. Worm drive axles were typical for the 1950s trucks.

A dark grey base coat was followed by a hairspray layer, then light grey that was washed away to create a worn and faded look.

5. The leaf springs and hangers were scratchbuild using Evergreen and Plastruct profiles.

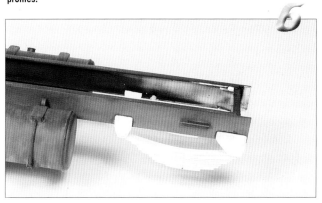

6. Here, the new springs have been installed. Note that there is no engine, but later a dummy drivetrain was mounted to fill the empty space.

7. Fine rusty chips were hand painted all over the frame with Vallejo acrylics.

89

so was the cab. They just didn't work together. Although the chassis was built for a different truck it could have been easily adopted for the Peterbilt cab; a generic CNC milled frame from KFS was used for this. It comes with parts for a couple of frame rails (which I did use in the exact length from the set) and generic cross members, of which I used just a few. There was some filling necessary but given how quickly it all came together the result was quite pleasing. The rear suspension is a good replica of the Page and Page unit I got from the same source as the cab, and I purchased it together with a pair of worm drive axles. No further research or scratch building on other chassis components was therefore necessary, and I just assembled what I had, with minor cleaning of the resin parts. The wheels I used came from another project , or which I have rebuilt older Italeri rims and tyres with a new tread. I sent this wheel for casting and planned to use it on various European projects I wanted to build. Due to the lack of suitable wheels I realised that if I modify the holes into a different shape, the rim will look like the old steel American rims – although it is technically not correct.

The Bubblenose cab is not tilting and therefore a detailed engine replica was not needed. The model ended up with a dummy engine and transmission I took from my spares box, from which barely the oil sump is visible, and no further details were required; just a prop shaft was connected to the rear axle. The pair of fuel tanks also came from my spares box, and I only made new mounting straps from

1. Both the truck and trailer wheels were painted the same way using the hair spray chipping technique.

2. The kit came with all the exterior and interior parts, including a wide choice of photo etched parts.

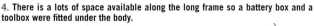

3. Mirror brackets were made of copper wire to replace the fragile resin castings.

4. There is a lots of space available along the long frame so a battery box and a toolbox were fitted under the body.

5. The 350 COE cab sits tall on the frame. The kit came with mounts and they fitted perfectly.

Evergreen rod. The front axle was also from another kit, while the front leaf springs and spring hangers were scratch built from different Evergreen profiles. The battery box on the right-hand side of the chassis was from a CTM PE set dedicated to Peterbilt 359 kits (the wing nuts come from the detail set for the Scania LB141) as well as the chassis steps; the left-hand-side box comes from the 350 kit. The fifth wheel is an AMT item taken from a scrapyard Peterbilt 359 kit and detailed with a sliding lock mechanism. Just

basic plumbing was added, as most of the frame would be hidden by the cab and the drom box. The rear lamps are of a simple rounded type with photo-etched lenses and milled aluminium frames I bought from Modelmakershop years ago.

The frame was primed with Mr.Surfacer 1200, followed by matt dark grey, and a fine coat of hairspray was applied, over which another fine coat of light grey was sprayed. Using a flat brush, the top grey coat was easily disturbed and chipped. The desired result

was to obtain a stained and patchy grey topcoat, rather than create any real chips. On this, small rusty chips were hand painted and the whole chassis received a few light dust filters and a bright wash around the details. Grease deposits and stains were applied around the fifth wheel, and the same dark grey was used on the tyres before they were masked, and the wheel centres were prepared for painting. The rims were sprayed with rust brown followed by hairspray, on which acrylic Tamiya XF-55 was applied and chipped again with a

1. PIE trucks were running with a pair of fog lights in the bumper. The holes were marked with a stencil and drilled out carefully.

2. Some spares box items were used on the model, such as the etched steps.

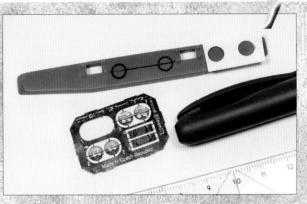

3. All the cab parts were primed with Mr.Surfacer 1200.

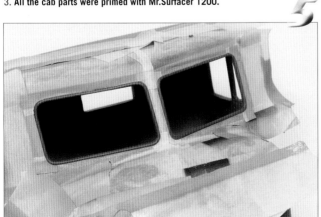

4. Tamiya acrylics were used for mixing the red PIE nuance.

5. Masking the window rubbers may be time consuming but when done properly, the painting takes just seconds.

6. Always make sure you have masked the surroundings properly to avoid any overspray.

water and a brush. One of the rims was painted flat white to add more interest. Rim chips were enhanced with rust oil paint tones, while a dark brown wash enlivened the wheel nuts.

8.3.2 THE CAB

All the cab parts come from the resin kit: the shell, interior, bumper, mudguards, rear cab mounts and the exhaust. The only one thing that must be added is the glazing and I made it all from clear Evergreen sheet. The interior consists of a floor on which the seats, dashboard and all the controls are attached. This assembly is fixed inside the cab shell once the latter is painted and windows are installed, and the floor fitted the cab perfectly. The original factory interior colour was brown, so I used a mixture of black and brown, and

sprayed all the parts this subsequent colour. Bright grey chips were then hand painted all around the seat bases and floor, but mostly remain hidden in the dark. The dashboard has useful PE details, and the gauges come printed on gloss paper and when covered with another PE panel with a convincing structure (that can be highlighted with sanding the top dark coat to reveal the gauge frames and controls) the dash looks perfect. Control levers were made from Evergreen rod and attached to the dashboard centre. I like the mirror arms to be realistically thin, so I did not use the resin parts, favouring my own efforts fashioned from copper wire. Although the kit contains two different grille versions (either fine mesh or vertical slats) the slats on the PIE trucks were horizontal. Luckily the correct part could

be sourced from the CTM White Freightliner set and the size was just about right.

The Wheels of Progress movie revealed that the PIE trucks had a pair of additional lights in the bumper. It only took me a minute to find out that a pair of suitable lamps can be taken from CTM's 24106 US Front Lights set. Using my punch-and-die set and plastic sheet, I made a stencil I to draw a pair of circles on the bumper where the lamps should be positioned. Using a drill and a round file and, following the marked lines, I made a pair of regular holes into which the lamps were inserted after painting. The headlights are out-of-box as a pair of CTM PE lights was already supplied in the kit. My chrome finish was rendered with Alclad II Chrome. The Peterbilt kit comes with great PE details; there are

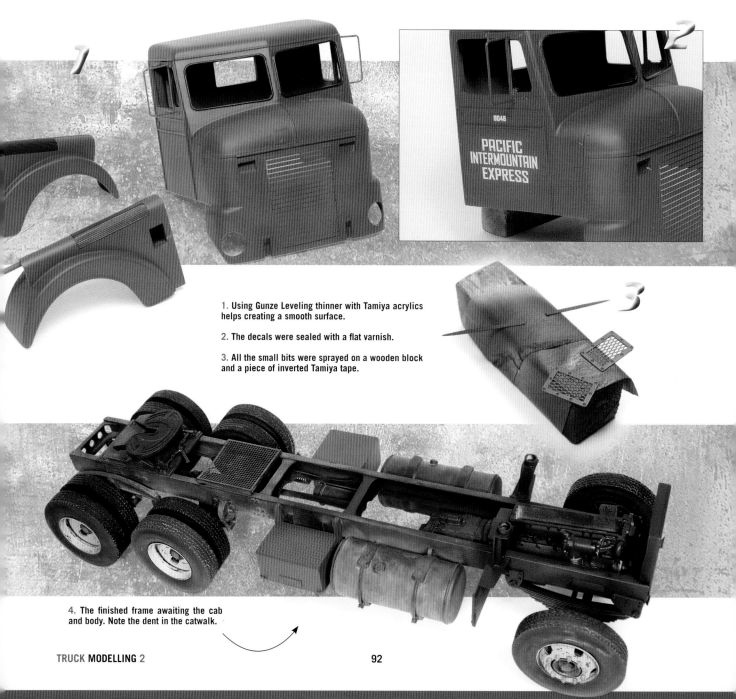

1. Using Gunze Leveling thinner with Tamiya acrylics helps creating a smooth surface.

2. The decals were sealed with a flat varnish.

3. All the small bits were sprayed on a wooden block and a piece of inverted Tamiya tape.

4. The finished frame awaiting the cab and body. Note the dent in the catwalk.

1. The Pete kit contained fine etched bits and pieces.

2. The interior is spartan but so was the real thing.

3. All parts were sprayed dark brown with bright contrasting chips but in the end, not much can be seen from it due to small windows.

convincing wipers and a realistic interior fan. Although it is a little too large in diameter, it looks great when assembled and fitted above the windscreen. A superb feature are the keys and key chain available on the fret as separate items. I placed a pair of the keys on a chain on the dashboard, together with a magazine and newspaper. There were no windows or cutting stencils in the cab, so measuring and cutting was required to make well-fitting glazing, which was secured with water-based white glue that dried clear – the benefits of that are obvious. For a better fit the side windows were split into two parts. Number plates came from the kit too and were painted the same as those fitted to a trailer.

There is a typical 50s cut-out on the cab rear right-hand-side corner, into which the exhaust silencer comes. The exhaust itself is an excellent one-piece casting together with the outlet pipe. There are two different versions of exhaust heat shields available in the kit and I plumped for the typical Peterbilt pattern. I originally thought this one was too modern for a truck of this type; however, I found period

photos showing very similar heat shields so I stick with what I'd selected and added rust effects.

8.3.3 THE BODY

The body behind the cab is what makes this tractor special and gives it the typical 50s look, as these bodies were frequently used by several operators back then. Building it was

quick and easy, but only because I have already built a similar body for the previous version of the model with the GMC cab. Therefore, I knew what material would be suitable, the pitfalls of scratch building a body of this size and the best way of assembling it.

93

There are two basic ways of constructing a general truck box body. You can either buy any of the available rigid truck or trailer kits to get the body, chop it to the desired length (or height) and close it with the rear door panel. The more difficult the body, the more time spent on modifications, which often result in extensive filling and sanding; both dirty and time-consuming. In this case, building a new body from sheet and profiles may be a more viable option and that is what I did on my Peterbilt. The body walls are made of ribbed sheets made by Evergreen. There are two sizes appropriate for this scale and I used the 4527 option. One pack is not usually enough for building a trailer, but for my body where the roof and rear door panels are flat, it was just about the right size.

While the suitable sheeting provides the wall surface structure, the other thing is that bodies such as this are not just square – the front wall and roof corners often being rounded for both a better look and the aerodynamics. As the PIE droms look more advanced and detailed, I just wanted something that would look accurate. It took me a while to figure how regular rounded corners could be achieved as Evergreen only offers rounded quarter rods up to 2.5mm. However, I had previous experience with cutting larger diameter plastic pipes into quarters to produce rounded corners. I therefore took the largest pipe Evergreen makes (12mm diameter), cut

1. Photo etched license plates were used.

2. They were then sprayed with a few layers of gloss white.

3. Individual colours were applied and sanded from the raised detail carefully.

4. The glazing was cut from clear styrene sheets and fixed with white glue.

5. With exterior details applied the cab was ready for installation.

6. All the chips were hanpainted with Vallejo acrylics. The dark ones were painted first.

7. Then the brighter surroundings were added. Note the reference pictures on page 39, pics 4 and 5.

TECH-TIP:
RUSTY EXHAUST PIPE

For generic rust I usually start building rust on a dark brown or black surface. On this I apply several transparent layers of rust colours (I use Lifecolor's Rust and Dust set) starting from the brightest to the darker tones. The initial layers I render with paints straight from the bottle, but for the upper layers I dilute these with water to make them more transparent and show the variations made in the previous steps. Once dry, usually in a few minutes, I apply multiple oil paint filters – shifting the final colour tone to my taste.

1 Back in the days the stacks were made of ordinary steel, no chrome, no aluminium and got all rusty easily.

2 The first rust layer I use is a dark brown primer.

3 Then a layer of the brightest rust tone from the Lifecolor set was applied. Note the random patern.

4 A piece of sponge was used instead of a brush to apply the Lifecolor acrylics for a more random rust structure.

DONE!
QUICK & EASY

PACIFIC INTERMOUNTAIN EXPRESS

5 Filters were then mixed from the acrylic paints and applied with a brush all over the exhaust.

1. Evergreen sheets and profiles were used for the completely scratch-built body.

2. The front corners were cut from a 12 mm Eevergreen pipe.

3. The body was sprayed silver, and the rear door light grey.

4. Tamiya masking tape and some paper sheets were used to mask the red stripe on the body.

5. Building the body was quick and took just a few hours. It was a lot quicker than rebuilding a body from any of the kits.

it in half and once again into a quarter section about 100mm long – enough for one vertical body corner. This way I got a pair of pleasing regular rounded corners with a 6mm radius. For the roof edges, 2.5mm quarter rod was just enough. The lower side wall edges were detailed with 4 x 1mm Evergreen strip with bolts cut from a hexagonal Plastruct rod, in an effort to follow the design of the dry van trailer. All the rear wall details, such as the door hinges and handles, were scratch built from Evergreen profiles. The trailer cables are made of a black rubber fibre and the air couplings and plug are scratch built, while the catwalk on the chassis is a CTM PE item taken from the White Freightliner set. Except for two pairs of marker lights from the AMT Ford C600 fitted to the side upper corners of the body, all the remaining marker lights and reflectors came from the CTM 24114 detail set. All these little embellishments help with the authenticity of the scratch-built body, which would otherwise look tot plain and simple.

Painting the drom was straightforward. The first layer was Mr.Finishing Surfacer Black. Mr.Color silver No.8 was used on the front and side walls, Tamiya Medium Grey was sprayed on the roof and lower side edges, and Mr.Color 97 Light Grey covered the rear door. Masking was employed for spraying each colour as well as for the red stripe all around. Black and dark brown oil paint filters were applied all around the body, but nothing too heavy as the original vehicles were maintained well. The front-upper left-hand corner of the body was weathered with soot pigments as there are always exhaust fume deposits in this area.

8.3.4 WEATHERING

The cab is the most distinctive part of the model, which received layered chips, dust and dirt/oil paint stains. As usual I started with primer. The main colour of the cab is red, so I used Grey Surfacer, which is bright enough for a standard red paint job. I blended Tamiya XF-7 Red and X-6 Orange to get closer to the red-orange tone seen in the Wheels of Progress movie. My intention was to achieve a satin surface rather than gloss, to which the oil paints would adhere badly. The door signwriting needed clear coat layers and sanding to hide the clear film edges. Then the cab shell interior was sprayed with dark brown and the window rubbers were masked with Tamiya tape and sprayed flat black.

Cab weathering comprised two layers of hand-painted chips. The first was painted red brown and the second bright red. Dark brown wash highlight all the panel lines and corners of the bodywork, and red filters were applied over the roof and hood panels. The dust effects were all hand painted with a fine brush using 502 Abteilung oils in multiple layers, and some speckling was added all around the model's lower areas to replicate dirt and mud splatters. The dirt on the windscreen was created with highly thinned oil paint applied over a stencil made from Tamiya masking tape. Once the paint was dry, the dirt effects can

1. Evergreen strips were utilised for scratch-building the hood latches.

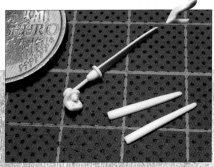

2. There were no indicator lights back then. Arms called trafficators were used to show the driving direction.

3. The trafficator was scratchbuilt and painted with silver and clear orange.

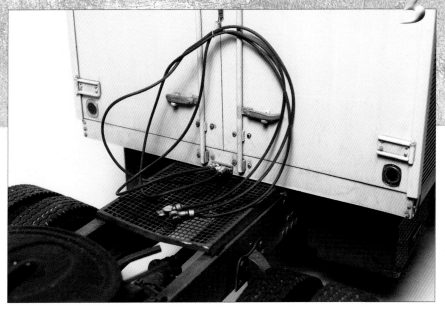

4. The finished part fitted on the cab.

5. Real rubber was used on the suzie lines on the back of the drom body, and the couplings were scratchbuilt.

The body drom body was weathered with oils. Note the exhaust soot on the roof.

1. A custom mixed red brown oil paint added shades into the corners all around the cab to increase dept.

2. Oil paint filters were applied over the lower body areas, and speckling was used to make the splashes. Vertical streaks were hand painted using a fine brush.

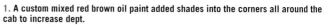

3-4. The windscreen was masked and weathered with thinned light dust oil paint.

be blended and refined with a dry brush. As the paint adhesion on gloss clear parts is limited, any corrections can be made easily. The exhaust was primed with Black Surfacer, over which Lifecolor rust paints were applied one after another. The next layer was a highly thinned filter made of the darkest Lifecolor rust tone, and a few drops of Italeri black acrylic paint, which ensured an authentic old rust tone. Bright flesh and rust tone oil paints were applied over the whole exhaust to reduce the colour uniformity.

CONCLUSION

The final truck and trailer combination in scale has been a dream of mine for many years. The model's size, well-known PIE livery and typical 50s combination makes this an eye-catching subject. The fact that I was not able to finish the original project only shows that sometimes our targets are higher than our skills. One has to be careful and think of this when planning a new project, because building one shelf queen after another gets frustrating. I have met quite a few modellers who disappeared from the scene, only because the complexity of the models they were building simply became too limiting. I fully understand that building a model should be challenging, but don't let this kill your passion. ▨

MODELLING

9 AMERICAN TRU

If you look at the International Prostar model described in first volume of this book series, you will probably agree that this is already an example of the "fibreglass era" fleet vehicle, which has most of the classic features already removed in the name of fuel efficiency, price and production costs.

Building such a model brings the modeller closer to completing a modern European truck with almost no chrome and a plain exterior. However, if you pick another box, one of the good old (or just old) AMT or Ertl kits, all the specifics of the classic American highway trucks are readily apparent.

THE VEHICLE ARCHITECTURE

When you become familiar with the world of American trucks and know something about how trucks are built outside of the US, the specifics of American design will quickly be obvious. It has to do with history and with how

things were done in the US in the past... differently. Since the early days of the trucking industry, the companies building trucks focused on producing and designing the vehicles themselves, but major sub-assemblies were purchased from suppliers. Effectively, they took the best engine and transmission, and the most suitable drive axles available, made their own frame and cab and built all the components into a vehicle. Different customers had distinct preferences, therefore it was common that your favourite truck make sported a wide choice of drivelines, axles and suspension systems so that eve-

ryone was able to get what they considered the best or the most suitable for their own application. Certain companies, such as Mack, were always proud to supply vehicles with their own driveline, and International did so too, but even here exceptions could be found.

Each vehicle that came of fthe assembly line was therefore specific and the level of possible customisation was very high. Something that was unheard of in Europe where everything is tied with laws, standards, mass production and where each truck producer usually makes their own engines and most

CK FEATURES

other components. Any rebuilding and modifying of the factory specification is so difficult in most European countries, that vehicles usually remain in the original configuration for their whole life. On the other hand, vehicles can be significantly rebuilt during their production life in the US. Yes, it is different nowadays compared what happened in the 1950s or 70s but there is still more freedom than in Europe. Obviously, more is possible in terms of conversions and accessories in the world of real American trucks and it is the same with building models.

Therefore, when constructing any European truck, the choice of components, configurations and dimensions is not unlimited. Often you are tied to factory specification, given wheelbase options and OEM components. On the other hand, when building American trucks, you can combine engines, transmissions, axles and many accessories, not speaking of the vehicle wheelbase. The older the vehicle the more freedom you have. Therefore, building 1950s trucks is not necessarily exhausting because often you can take the engine there, the axles there, the fuel tank here, scratch-build the frame and add various bits and pieces from the spares box and it will look good. It still may not be 100% accurate, but it is still easier than building European trucks from any period. No engine issues, no concerns with wheel hubs and no big deal with the wheelbase either. What a dream!

What is often discussed with American trucks is length limits. I often hear there are no length limits and never were in the US, and that American rigs can be as long as desired… but that is far from reality. There have always been length limits and they were often differed between states. Yes, in the US most restrictions are related to trailer length and, therefore, using long conventional tractors is not a problem. However different states also had different length limits for various truck and trailer combinations. In some places, double and triple trains were allowed, but they were illegal elsewhere, and it was similar for various forms of equipment. These limits shaped the equipment employed in

different states. Western trucks were always different from those used on the east coast. It was the overall length limit that gave birth to all those various 'bubblenose' tractors in the fifties, which benefited from having the cab high above the engine to maximise the cargo compartment length – and it was also the reason why cabover trucks were popular in some decades. Of course, length limits have been changing over the years and they went from short trailers over what most AMT kits allow (40ft trailers) and then to 48ft later and to the current federal standard which is 53ft of the semitrailer length.

Vehicle architecture in the case of cabover tractors (COE, i.e. cab-over-engine) is not that far from what is common in Europe. A specific feature is that many vehicles were available in two configurations: as a set-forward axle version and set-back, this being valid for both cabover trucks and conventio-

nal examples. Logically the set-forward axle vehicles have just a minimal front overhang, while the axle on set-back vehicles is moved rearwards, similarly to most European trucks. The benefits of the different configurations are higher payloads or the needsto meet some specific limits in weight distribution or increased manoeuvrability (set-back) vs better riding comfort (set-forward).

Conventional tractor architecture is very different from what we are used to in Europe. The classic layout comprises a hood of a certain length (while the length from the bumper to the back of the cab = BBC is used to classify hood length from short over the standard, long and extended). Behind the hood there is a cab that is quite narrow (not much wider than the hood) so there is just enough space for a pair of seats with a small gap between. On modern trucks the cabs are getting wider, but the old conventional cabs are

A modern truck, but with all the classic features. The International Lonestar still features dual air cleaners, a pair of vertical stacks, chrome bumper and aluminium fuel tanks and battery boxes.

not any wider than a regular passenger car. On a day cab vehicle there is just this narrow and short cab. On a long-haul example (as the cab itself is very small), additional driver quarters are necessary, and these are called sleepers. Long ago, additional sleepers appeared on trucks located behind the cab that were wide enough to have a bunk inside, so the driver could sleep comfortably. Sleepers were available in various lengths and makes (often these were custom units provided by dedicated suppliers, such as Double Eagle and Mercury) and were accessible either from the outside through a side doo, or via an opening in the cab rear wall. Later, large integral sleeper cabs appeared which were long and high cabs that came in one piece with the sleeper area. Some early versions of integral cabs were already seen in the 1950s on Mack or Autocar tractors or maybe even earlier. However, certain manufacturers still offer classic cabs with separate sleepers, equipped with a larger opening in the rear cab wall, which makes the sleeper more accessible from the driver's seat.

MATERIALS AND TECHNOLOGY

If there is something special and typical about classic American highway trucks, it is the amount of lightweight and non-corrosive materials used. The wide employment of aluminium for building heavy trucks is unique; the material not being used widely anywhere else on the world. It dates to the 1950s when aluminium was used not just for cabs and rims in a larger scale, but also on frames and various chassis parts. Later, together with fiberglass, this meant that despite their size the American trucks were mostly lighter than their European counterparts where steel and cast iron are still the most typical building materials. The use of aluminium is also tied with riveting as, after the war, this was the

A typical 1950s drivetrain that consists of a main four speed speed and auxiliary three speed transmission. The main is bolted on the engine bellhousing while the auxiliary is separate, connected with a prop shaft.

most common and cheapest technology for producing all kinds of aluminium bodywork. Not only cabs, but whole trailers were typically built of aluminium.

Stainless steel was used for structural components such as various mounts or parts exposed to higher mechanical stress or higher temperatures. Bumpers, exhausts, mirrors and other components were typically made of stainless steel or chromed steel, instead of aluminium.

Modern aerodynamic vehicles have lost many classic features, as both aluminium and stainless steel are expensive. Therefore, plastic

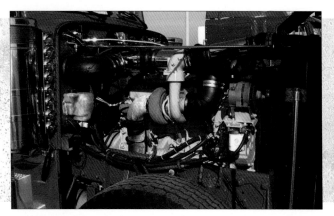

A 3406B Caterpillar engine in a 379 Peterbilt. This engine is probably the finest and most popular on-highway engine Caterpillar has ever made. Note the typical Cat engine yellow.

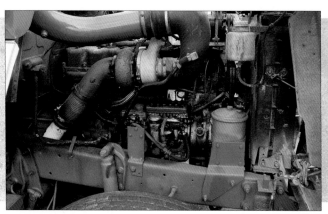

One of the few companie who kept using their own engines was Mack such as this ENDT 675 turbocharged diesel.

The 71 series Detroit Diesel two stroke engines are a true classic for anything from 50s till at least mid 70s (6V-71 in the picture). They were typically green, however the tone in the picture is not very authentic.

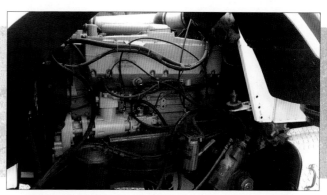

A common feature of the Cummins engines is the aftercooler (a large water-to-air charge air cooler) mounted on the cylinder head. The cream colour was typical for the 70s and 80s era .

and fiberglass are now widely employed as a lightweight and cost-saving material, while many traditional features such as chromed exhausts, mirrors, air horns and marker lights are often removed in the name of cost, efficiency and aerodynamics.

EXHAUSTS

Another typical feature of an average US truck is its exhaust. A typical exhaust is normally placed along the cab sides on a conventional vehicle, or behind it on a cabover, and consists of a silencer, and heat shield, and may also have a rain cap incorporated at the end of the outlet pipe. The heat shield provides protection from any contact with the exposed hot surfaces and avoids driver injury. While the exhaust is one of the most typical features, times are changing and modern vehicles often have just a very simple and non-decorative single exhaust stack – or have just a horizontal exhaust under the frame just like their European counterparts. Another interesting fact is that some of the latest trucks that preserve the typical dual exhausts have just one of them working, while the other is just a dummy to maintain vehicle symmetry.

ROOF MARKERS AND CHICKEN LIGHTS

American trucks are well known for their decorative marker lights. The so-called 'bullet lights' have regularly appeared on trucks since the 1960s but can be seen on much older vehicles, in a somewhat different shape. The usual number of these lights is five – one on each cab side and three in the middle. They mostly consist of a clear orange lens and a chromed housing. The moniker chicken lights refers to all other marker lights placed on a vehicle – cab sides, bumpers, air filters, mirror brackets and so on. These are now easy to replicate on a model as CTM has a wide array of many common shapes and sizes, and from different periods.

A pair of vertical exhaust stacks. With or without a silencer, and covered with a heat shield, this is the most typical feature of a classic American truck.

SLIDING 5TH WHEELS

While in Europe the 5th wheel position is typically fixed, a sliding 5th wheel is a long-time common feature on American trucks. It concerns being able to change the length of your truck and trailer combination and changing the weight distribution on individual axles. In the US, there is a mathematical expression called 'bridge formula', used to determine the vehicle gross weight depending on the number and position of the axles. Therefore, being able to position the 5th wheel means you can make your vehicle fit easily within the limits, with different loads. A similar feature, a sliding semitrailer undercarriage, is also a common feature, which also helps with weight distribution within the bridge formula and improves manoeuvrability.

In the case of the sliding 5th wheel, the mounting plate is significantly longer to allow the 5th wheel to move back and forth – and contains a pair of toothed racks used to define the sliding path, and secure the 5th wheel in position. The locking mechanism is usually air operated and the whole movement can be executed from the cab. You just unlock the fifth wheel sliding mechanism, apply the parking brake, and let the tractor drive a few inches to the desired 5th wheel position. In the same way, with a trailer parking brake applied and the undercarriage mechanism released, the trailer axle position can be changed.

HEADACHE RACKS AND POGO STICKS

There are other standout components on American trucks that make them different: pogo sticks and headache racks among them.

A 'pogo stick' is a vertical rod fitted on the frame behind the cab, carrying both air and electrical trailer lines. It originates from older times when the hose and cables were only available in a straight line and not coiled. These hanged on springs on the top of the stick, providing free hose and cable length to allow extension during cornering. Even now, with the coiled hose and cables that supply this function, a pogo stick is often installed on a vehicle.

A headache rack is a safety cab guard installed on the vehicle frame just behind the cab, protecting the vehicle from any damage in case the load shifts during any emergency (a crash or sudden braking). This is typically employed on trucks pulling flatbed trailers as these usually have no front wall, which would do the job and protect the vehicle (unlike in Europe where the trailer front wall usually has this function). There are many types of these guards, from steel to aluminium and in various finishes from stainless, aluminium to standard painted steel. These racks often do not act just as protection, but also have various lockers, toolboxes, chain or tie-down hangers or even hydraulic oil tanks built in.

LUBE FINERS

This is a small cylindrical vessel on classic US trucks, mounted somewhere close to the engine, usually on the cab side wall or over the mudguard (on a conventional) or somewhere on the frame, usually near the battery box (on a cabover). It's an additional bypass oil filter that works together with standard engine oil filters, to preserve oil quality and reduce engine mechanical wear – and extends the oil exchange intervals. The vessel holds a filter cartridge that can be replaced, just like any other filter, and it is connected with the engi-

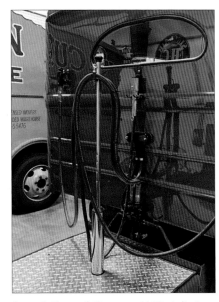

A so called 'pogo stick' - a support fot the trailer hose and cables - have been used since 50s.

Straight hoses and cables are sometimes weaved into decorative shapes.

Orange bullet shaped roof marker lights have been a classic feature for nearly 60 years now.

The sliding 5th wheel mechanism is usually operated with an air cylinder. Note the coiled air hose.

One of the earlier alternatives of the rook marker lighs are those mounted on a B series Mack.

A tooth rack on the base plate was used for guiding the 5th wheel and defining its individual positions.

Hood emblems have been popular with some brands. This is the classic Peterbilt, while Mack had their typical bulldog.

A headache rack has usually two functions. It is a heavy duty cab protection but often it serves for storage of chains and all sorts of tie downs.

Externally mounted lubefiners were often chromed and displayed proudly on the cab sides.

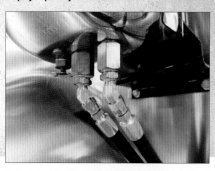

Note that the lubefiner has a drain valve and a pair of fittings for the inlet and outlet at the bottom.

Air cleaners, often dually mounted with one on each side of the hood, is another common feature on the classic trucks.

On some trucks the air cleaner was just a single one and it was not necessarily aluminium but painted steel as shown on this 358 Peterbilt.

Auxiliary power units are common on modern American trucks. These supply electric power for the the vehicle- and AC when parked.

ne lubrication circuit with a pair of hose, one feeding the lube finer with oil and the other returning oil back to the engine. The finish can be both chromed, or painted.

AIR INTAKE FILTERS

It is important to note that what is just a simple sheet metal vessel hidden deep underneath the cab on most European trucks, has become an important visual feature on many American conventional haulers. These trucks historically kept their air intake filters outside the hood, usually mounted vertically on the cab side near the engine firewall. Either there was a single filter mounted on one side and a lube finer on the opposite side of the cab or dual filters, one on each vehicle side, and the lube finer was installed on the chassis between the wheel arch and battery box. The filters, visible and accessible for easy maintenance, became the subject of detailing. Chromed, stainless or polished aluminium, and customised with various chicken lights, the filters themselves became a classic feature and a common decoration of big American highway trucks. These features are common to American and Australian trucks. What is special about trucks in Australia is that the intake pipes are raised high above the cab roof to prevent the engine breathing dust and dirt while on outback roads, and to allow the vehicle to ford rivers or flooded areas.

ELECTRICAL SYSTEM

While European trucks typically operate with 24-Volt system and use a pair of 12V batte-

ries, American trucks employ a 12-Volt system; a common configuration is four 6V batteries.

WHEELS

The wheels on American trucks (and the rims in particular) are a typical feature. In the US, more than anywhere else, aluminium rims are widely used while in Europe, for example, this is considered an expensive custom feature that not everybody can afford. Not only that, it adds to the volume of aluminium used in the vehicle structure and reduces weight of a typical American truck, but also matches the use of polished aluminium, stainless and chrome on other vehicle components, making the vehicle shiny.

Aluminium wheels were first made by Alcoa in 1948. Back then these were the old split-rim wheels with tube tyres and typically five small holes. Later in the 1960s, the rim design changed into the ten-hole type, but the rims were still of the split variety with tube tyres. These rims are available in most AMT and Ertl kits. Tubeless tyres and rims appeared during the '60s and became increasingly popular, slowly replacing the split-rim design. Over the years they came in different shapes and sizes (22in, 24in) and became a somewhat standard feature for most vehicles.

Except for aluminium rims, standard pressed-sheet metal rims have been used in the US. The early designs were of the split-rim type with five or six holes. As tubeless tyres arrived the typical white two-hole tubeless rims became standard and have been used ever since on cheaper large fleet vehicles, such as delivery trucks or day cab tractors.

Except for the steel and aluminium disc wheels, the typical spyder wheels (called Dayton type, spoke or Trilex wheels) have been used in the US, too. They again come in various shapes and designs, including both the tube and tubeless tyres and are also a typical item in Australia.

What is very special about the wheels of all American trucks is the difference in the wheel stud pitch circle diameter. While in Europe the pitch is 10x335 (ten holes on the pitch circle 335mm), US trucks have the bolt circle diameter of 285.75mm. The resulting difference of 50mm on the pitch circle diameter is clearly visible and has a significant impact on the rim overall shape and look. Therefore, US and European truck rims are not interchangeable. You can easily identify European components used on some US-operated vehicles, typically busses that employ European axles with the 10x335 pitch.

NUMBER PLATES AND PERMITS

While it might seem that trucking in the US was easy and free of regulations and limits in the past (compared to Europe), it has never been that simple. Different states had varying weight and length limits, required different

Modern American trucks, especially those from larger fleets, are often streamlined with additional deflectors and wheel covers.

This is an old 60s 22 inch tube type, split rim Alcoa wheel which are often found in AMT kits. Note that it is clean, but still completely dull and flat. This is what happens when the aluminium is not polished regularly.

This is an 80s version of the tubeless polished aluminium Alcoa 22,5 inch rim. You can find these in the Revell and Monogram kits.

Some highway trucks in the past used the huge 24,5 inch rims. It is basically the same type of rim as in the previous picture but significantly larger in diameter.

The same type of rim as shown above, just mounted on the steer axle. Note that the rim itself and the outer ring are aluminium while the spring is steel.

Dayton type wheels are an alternative to the classic budd wheels. They came as both the split rim and tubeless versions.

It was not rare to see that highway trucks produced between 50s and 70s lacked brakes on the front axles.

A modern alternative to twin mounted wheels are these super singles, now commonly used on both truck and trailers. Note the aluminium wheel hub.

Modern IFTA stickers. Note that each year has a different colour.

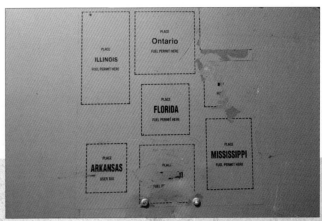

The large truck operators had their trucks prepared for the fuel permit stickers. Compare the blank fields for Illinois, Florida, Arkansas and Ontario with the permits in the picture below.

Multiple license plates were typical for the highway trucks between 50s and 70s. Note the bingo plate in the centre.

The old-style fuel permits with individual designs for different states used before the unified IFTA stickers were introduced.

Back in the days, sanders were used on trucks to increase adhesion of the drive wheels. The same equipment was offered by Volvo and Scania too and a similar principle is still used in Scandinavia.

Simple mudflaps with different safety signs or logos have been typical for American trucks.

permits and demanded different taxes. Therefore, many trucks (especially those in the 1950s-60s) carried multiple number plates and were registered in different states due to tax benefits. Some of these plates were local state permits. Due to various laws, different permits (fuel, ICC, tax) have appeared in the form of a sticker that drivers placed on their cab sides. In the past, the fuel permits were separate for each individual state, which resulted in so-called 'bingo plates' being fitted to trucks, on which the different stickers were placed. This has been replaced by the IFTA permit used today, which is agreed by 48 states and some Canadian provinces.

The difference in number plate use still common today, is that in some states, having two number plates, both the front and rear, is mandatory – while others require just one number plate, either the front or rear example.

CONCLUSION

As you can see, there are some specifics originating from American trucking history that had an impact on the way US trucks were designed and built. Some disappeared over time, while others became traditional and are still seen today; however, their function is no longer necessarily vital. Please, don't expect this chapter to be an exact or a complete guide. While similar at first sight, the vehicles still differ in detail so the information just provided may not apply to every single example. ■

10 PETERBILT 359
-BUILDING A CLASSIC AMERICAN TRUCK

The 359 Peterbilt is a classic. Building one has always been a dream of mine and I definitely wanted to have one in the book. What inspired me was a Youtube video where a short wheelbase 359 tractor was introduced as a vehicle rebuilt from a single drive model, and now being operated as a recreational vehicle. I liked the typical old paint scheme and thought it would look good as a model. Armed with the latest CTM photo-etched sets for the AMT Peterbilt kit, I decided to give it a try.

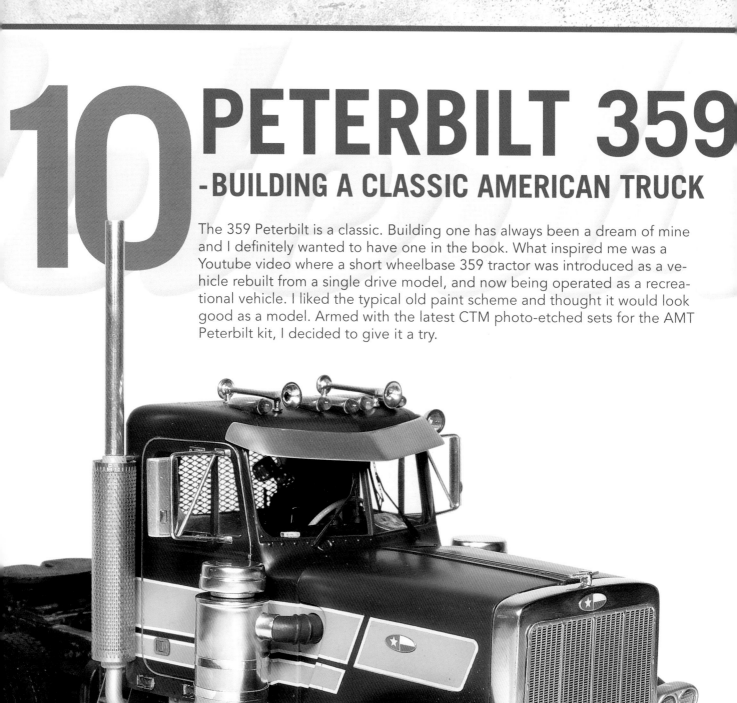

10.1 INTRODUCTION

I already had a finished 359 in my display case, which was pretty pleasing, but over time I thought I would give it one more try and sort out some of the kit issues I failed to tackle during the first attempt. So, I put my 359 into pieces carefully and started building it again. What I didn't like were the wheels and the hood alignment to both the cab and the bumper. Changing the wheels was not an issue, thanks to beautiful rims and tyres from Jamie Rahmoeller (www.moluminum. com). However, the latter caused me a slight

headache and a lots of conversion work. Trying to make the model look better almost turned the work in progress into an unfinished 'shelf queen', and it was all more difficult than expected. It finally took me more than a year to finish my Peterbilt although the original plan was to spend just a couple of months on it.

10.2. FRAME AND CHASSIS ASSEMBLY

The AMT kits come from the golden age of truck modelling. Many new products were entering the market back then and the range

of models available was expanding rapidly. However, this was more than 40 years ago and what was deemed standard moulding quality back then is considered rather poor today. There are no new kits to replace the old versions, so model builders still need to work with the aging 1970s tooling. Some of the basic parts in AMT kits are decent, but others are rough and need much improvement. It is not unusual to throw away certain kit components and replace them to expedite the build.

That is what I did when building the model all those years ago. I scratch-built the frame and converted it to the day cab. The framework was still good, and I still liked the day cab look, so the only major thing I had to do was to cut down the wheelbase. I also replaced the upper horizontal section of the frame with thicker Evergreen strip, as the vehicle I

TECH SPEC
Peterbilt 359

Kit: AMT Peterbilt 359
Scale: 1:25
Accessories: CTM 033 AMT Peterbilt detail set, CTM 24154 Peterbilt painted dash, CTM 24092 tail lights, CTM 24108 Front lights, CTM 24093 Orange marker lights, Moluminum rims and tyres.
Notes: Wheelbase cut and sleeper removed, Detroit Diesel engine from AMT GMC Astro kit with 8V92 style rocker covers from Double Take Replicas

1. This 359 was built long ago but it was too attractive to be thrown away.

2. Shortening the wheelbase was the first modification.

3. Next up was rebuilding the hood hinges to get rid of the large gaps between the bumper and mudguards.

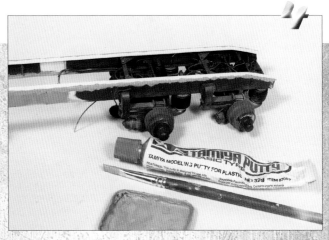

4. All the filling on the frame was done with Tamiya putty thinned with acetone.

5. Priming was done with my favourite Mr.Surfacer 1200.

was now building had an aluminium frame. You can always tell the steel and aluminium frame apart by two features. First, the aluminium parts have much thinner walls than the steel examples. Second, all the chips on the aluminium frame are bright, exposing the silver-coloured metal underneath that does not suffer from corrosion in the same way as steel.

The front axle in most of these old kits is not steerable. I converted mine by carefully cutting the original axle into pieces and adding pins to it. The rest of the axles and suspension was mostly built as per the instructions. The wheels in the oldest AMT kits look too small, so I replaced them with modern and well-detailed hubs, rims and wheels from Moluminum. The truck has a somewhat unusual layout of chassis components due to its short wheelbase, as there is simply not enough space, but I quite liked it. The fuel tank comes from the Italeri Volvo F12 (AMT originals being too small) and the added straps hail from CTM's detail set. The battery box and frame

steps were taken from the same set and simply folded and fitted to the frame rails. The fact that the PE parts were nickel plated saved much time as they do not have to be painted. Mud flaps with mounts again were from CTM 's PE fret, but this offers a mix of parts for the 1/25 359 AMT and 1/24 378 Italeri kits. The sliding 5th wheel is straight from the kit but had the base plate modified and detailed with the sliding mechanism air lock. The pogo stick, three trailer lines made of rubber fibre

and the air/electric coupling were all scratch-built and taken directly from the previously constructed model.

The wiring concept is the same I use all the time. It is made from KFS white metal air valves and mostly lead and copper wires. I have also added scratch-built load-sensing valves for the brake system. To enhance the wiring when rebuilding the model, I decided to add two new bundles and extend the wiring along the whole length of the chassis.

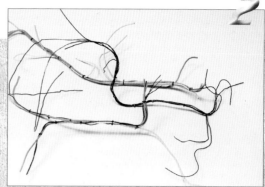

1. The original model had no wiring in the engine compartment so I added few bundles in this area.

2. Each of the bundle was prepared separately outside of the chassis using CTM cable ties.

10.3 POWER

I wanted the engine in this model to be a little special. The original kit has a Cummins NTC but I replaced it with two-stroke Detroit Diesel 8V92, echoing the truck I was using as a reference. Some of the AMT kits contain the older 8V71 engine, which I converted into 8V92 adding the typical square rocker covers from Double Take Replicas, which is the most distinctive feature apart from some other details on the block and heads. The basic engine was built following the kit instructions and the modifications I made lie mostly in the details and accessories added. I have used some engine components (turbocharger, air compressor, alternator) from my own resin supplies. The engine also received styrene bolt heads and I also scratch-built clamps on the exhaust piping. The typical flat vertical section of the exhaust manifold, which runs down along the right-hand side of the engine, was fashioned from styrene sheet and profile, and detailed with welds made from a piece of styrene fibre melted by Tamiya Extra Thin glue. Rough, rust texture was replicated by tapping a brush with Mr.Surfacer 500 on the surface. The transmission was left as it was just with some bolt heads added. The prop shafts were scratch built with all the universal joints made from plastic strip and detailed with resin bolt heads. I re-worked the original kit radiator

1. The basic engine received many resin add-ons. The rocker covers helped me to convert the 8v-71 into a 8v-92.

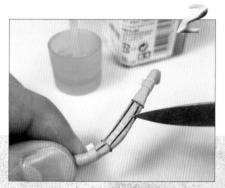

2. Stretched sprue was applied for weld seams, melted with glue and then shaped with a scalpel.

3. As the engine got the turbocharger all the inlet and exhaust piping had to be scratchbuilt.

4. The typical flat exhaust section helps to pass around the front wheel on the passenger side of the frame.

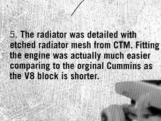

5. The radiator was detailed with etched radiator mesh from CTM. Fitting the engine was actually much easier comparing to the orginal Cummins as the V8 block is shorter.

TRUCK MODELLING

1. I always start the HS chipping method with dark rust primer followed by the chipping medium.

2. A very important step in HS chipping is to use a suitable paint. Tamiya acrylics are the best ones.

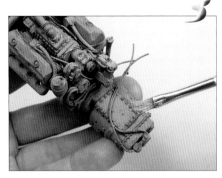

3. Once the paint is fully cured, you can slowly start chipping the edges and exposed details with a wet brush.

4. I used the original Tamiya paint to highlight the edges of some of the chips with a brighter green.

5. The whole assembly was treated with dark wash to highlight all the details and add depth and contrast.

6. The first layer of rust was hand painted with Vallejo acrylics and enhanced with pigments.

7. The irregular fresh rust were made with pigments and the speckling method.

8. The 8v-92 Detroit as many of the drivers and mechanics know them. It's often nicknamed "The Green leaker" due to frequent oil leaks or "Screaming Jimmy" for its typical two stroke, high frequent sound. There are more differences between the 8v-92 and 8v-71 than just the square rocker covers, but for a 1/25 scale replica it's most obvious one.

and embellished it with bolt heads and a filling cap. The core was cut out and replaced with fine PE radiator mesh from CTM.

10.4 CAB INSIDE OUT

The cab is a one-piece shell which is typical for 1/25 scale kits. Its hood is in one piece, to which the mudguards and radiator grille are attached. It's all simple but the model's previous life revealed that the hood sits a little too high and that there is a gap between the

grille/mudguards and bumper, which should not be there. The finished model had rather an off-highway look while the on-highway 359 usually sits quite low. I therefore lowered the cab on the frame as much as possible, along with the front axle. All this resulted in rebuilding the hood hinges, to allow the hood to tilt with minimal clearance to the bumper. The gap between the bumper and fenders was reduced and the hood-cab fit was im-

proved. It may sound quick and straightforward, but I am not sure I'd be willing to go through the process again!

The cab modifications involved replacing the moulded handles with CTM photo-etched examples. I also added a frame around the door aperture; this is missing in many AMT kits so I spent time thinking about making a replacement that looked good and did not have to be painted, as it would be tricky. I decided to insert 0.8mm solder wire into the panel line around the cab door, and fixed it

1. The hood went through some significant modifications to ensure it fitted the cab properly.

2. Framing was made from soldering wire.

3. Reworking the hood hinges and making the hood open smoothly was a tricky task.

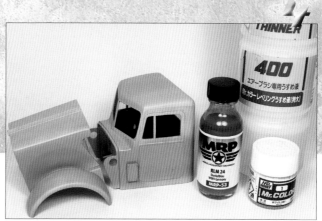

4. The light blue area under the stripes was sprayed first.

5. The etched grille was test fitted on the hood before painting.

6. Once dry the stripes were carefully masked with Tamiya tape.

7. I like the Mr.Paint colour tones a lot. However, it needed suprisingly many layers to get a decent opaque dark blue coat.

9. The grille chrome was also done with Mr.Paint chrome. The white pin stripes are KFS decals.

8. I always enjoy unmasking after the paintjob. Patient masking will ensure a great finish.

1. The original AMT bath tub interior was cut to pieces. Floor and roof panels were scratchbuilt.

2. CTM makes fine etched cell phones with holders. They come in different types and colours.

3. As I was not putting my 359 back to the 80s I was happy to use the cell phone in the interior.

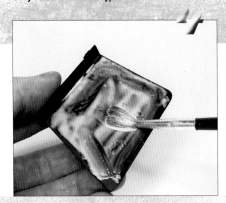

4. White glue was applied on the floor before flocking.

5. A kitchen strainer was used to apply an even layer of the powder.

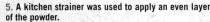

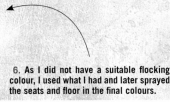

6. As I did not have a suitable flocking colour, I used what I had and later sprayed the seats and floor in the final colours.

with cyanoacrylate glue, before the panel line around the door was then made with a razor. The firewall was scratch built with wiring and fuse boxes added and, once painted, KFS data plate decals were added. The grille frame was sanded and a hole was cut where the original plastic mesh was moulded to provide space for the CTM etched grille.

I sourced air cleaners from a diecast Revell Peterbilt 359. The AMT kit has just a small single cleaner, while my references showed large double cleaners. The mounts for these had to be scratch built and carefully aligned on the cab, while the inlet manifold matching the new cleaners was a homespun item, except for the rubber elbows, whch again came from the diecast 'Pete'. After painting, the cleaners were glued using 5-minute epoxy – to allow alignment time – and fitted with mounting straps made from thin aluminium sheet. The exhaust silencer was built from Evergreen tube, the outlet pipe a polished aluminium version fashioned from K&S metal and the heat shield came from the CTM PE set.

Mirror brackets were scratch built from Evergreen rod as the kit parts were too thick, while the air horns were replaced with items from an Italeri Scania 143. Roof marker lights came via the kit and are reasonable. All the 'jewellery' was coloured with Alclad applied over gloss black paint, and the lights, except for roof markers, were provided by the sets made by CTM – including the orange markers all around the cab, hood and bumper, which added extra realism.

The interior of this model was rebuilt significantly and detailed with many add-ons. Normally the AMT kits come with the interior formed as a 'bathtub'. The floor and side wall details form one part, which fails to align properly with the upper shell, so I cut the 'tub' in pieces and almost only the door panel was used. Styrene sheet of 1mm thickness replicated the floor. And the interior was upgraded with a full treatment of CTM PE. The major improvement is the two-layer dashboard, which comes pre-painted and all you must do is to stick it in place.

One factor with most kits is that the pedals are simplified. Given this moulding was from the 1970s, it was basic and sparsely detailed. CTM, however, offers replacement components to boost the authenticity. The PE pedals are beautiful and have a very fine structure, made just for a light wash to highlight their structure. Brake and accelerator pedals sit on the floor and the clutch is the famous massive steel lever, which I made from a copper wire. The roof panel was scratch built from styrene sheet and detailed with sun visors and an

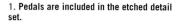

1. Pedals are included in the etched detail set.

2. Revised interior ready for assembly.

3. Mud and dust pigments were used to weather the boots.

4. New firewall was scratch-built to replace the poor kit part.

5. Details on the firewall were picked out with a brush, and a few KFS data plates and warning signs were added.

interior light. On the cab rear wall, a soft styrene sheet supplied by Denmark's H.A. Models was employed, being carefully cut into shape and painted the same colour as the door panels. Not only does this material possess a pleasing padded structure but is soft, and therefore can easily be formed around a curved surface. Flocking powder was used on the seats and floor. This is normally available for model car builders and made by different companies in various colours. I used a brush to apply white glue over the parts and covered them with flocking, spreading it with a fine strainer. This was repeated twice, so the layer was uniform and had the desired opacity. The structure was somehow fine,

but the colour was not what I planned, so I decided to spray the floor grey and the seats blue.

Once the basic parts were finished, I have added everyday 'junk'; the dice hung in the cab were made from hand moulded Miliput Superfine White, and the dots produced by a 0.5mm drill. Floor mats were replicated by CTM Peterbilt mud flaps, cut to size and detailed with Peterbilt logos. The cell phone and its holder on the dash came from a CTM 24002 cell phone detail set, while the cigarette boxes and magazines were graphics made on a computer, scaled down, printed, cut out and folded. The gear stick was detailed with airline and PE cable ties, and the boots were an

item acquired from a friend some time ago. Both the lifting jack and an oil can are scratch built. The cab glazing was made of clear styrene sheet, the wipers being from KFS. The rear window guard is actually a catwalk from a larger 1/24 scale Peterbilt PE package.

10.5 ADDING COLOUR

Painting this model was a combination of two worlds. Weathering the engine and chassis was one and traditional for me. The smooth and shiny metallic parts, however, was another that needed much more patience and care. I had a good idea about the model's final look since the early building stages: clean and original paint that is still neat, but

TECH-TIP:
CHROMED METAL

Painting chrome surfaces is generally considered difficult and many modellers struggle with their results. American trucks are popular in modelling but the chrome in the kits is usually of poor quality, so it is hard to avoid painting chrome. But the whole process is relatively easy and straightforward. It can be split into the main four steps shown in the following photos. Where most modellers fail is in the very first step – ensuring a clean and glossy surface. The rest is easy, as Alclad II Chrome itself is very user friendly and comes in bottles pre-mixed and ready for spraying.

1 Step one for Alclad chrome or any similar chrome paint is a perfectly cured and clean gloss black surface.

2 Imperfections can be sanded and polished if needed. Any dust or dirt on the model would be highlighted by the chrome.

3 Toothpicks are very useful for handling small parts during spraying.

4 Alclad paints need a little extra fine polishing after spraying.

A shiny polished aluminium (not chrome in fact) surface is one of the elementrary classic American truck features.

DONE!
QUICK & EASY

no longer glossy, and the aluminium frame covered with bright chips of the dark paint, exposing the silver material of the frame rails. The blue cab colours were from Mr.Paint as I quite liked the tones, the rest is mostly Mr.Color and Tamiya acrylics with Vallejo used for hand painting the smallest details. As far as the metallic paints are concerned, I have used more options on a trial basis: Alclad II Chrome, Spaz Stix, Mr.Paint chrome and Molotow Liquid Chrome.

The cab and hood were first painted light blue (with a few drops of Mr.Color white), the stripes were masked, and the rest of the cab sprayed dark blue. Mr.Paint's shades were easy to use as they come pre-mixed in the bottles. The individual paint layers were quite transparent, so more were required for an opaque result, but the masked area's edges were sharp, and the final surface pleasingly

smooth and fine. The white stripes came from the KFS decal sheet and were sealed with Mr. Color semi-gloss varnish. Windscreen rubbers were hand painted with Vallejo acrylics. Then, after the cab was sprayed with dark blue, the only thing I had to do was to use a fine san-

ding stick and abrade all the paint from the wire frame, exposing the bright metal surface underneath.

The Mr.Paint hues are also suitable for the hairspray technique. I have seen quite a lot of 1960s and 70s trucks with the aluminium on

1. The light housings were treated with Molotow Liquid chrome.

2. A few fingerprints were repaired by spraying Spaz Stix on the air cleaners after fitting them to the cab.

3. The air cleaners actually come from a Revell die-cast Peterbilt and were rebuilt to fit the AMT 359.

4. As the frame was all aluminium, silver was used under the chipping medium instead of a traditional dark rust.

5. The chassis assembly was quite complex so the spraying was done in steps. I usually spray all the internal areas first.

6. The Mr.Paint colours need a little different approach for chipping as they are more resistant to water.

7. Most of the chipping on the frame was done with a scalpel on the wet surface.

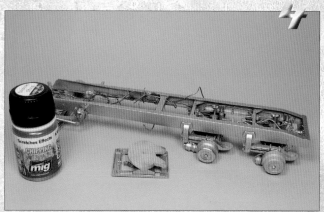

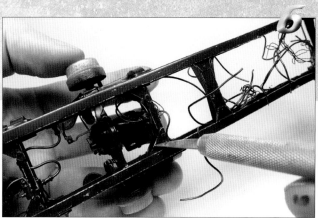

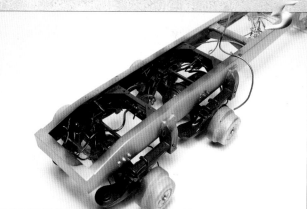

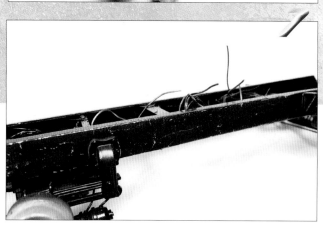

1. Black oil paint was applied in a rearward direction, to mimic traces of a trailer sliding down from the fifth wheel.

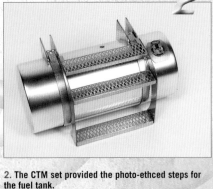

2. The CTM set provided the photo-etched steps for the fuel tank.

3. Fine airbrush filters were used to weather the chassis lower areas, suspension and axles.

the frame rails exposed by old paint peeling in layers, revealing the bright aluminium underneath: I wanted this effect on my model too. Therefore, I sprayed the frame with Mr.Color silver, applied two layers of Ammo Chipping fluid and let them dry. Next was a fine but opaque layer of Mr.Paint dark blue. The chipping was carried out with water and all sorts of tools. It needed more rubbing compared to

Tamiya acrylics, but it worked well and was quite easy to create small and fine chips – and keep the result under control. The engine was also chipped using the hairspray technique, the coat of light green being mixed from Tamiya acrylics.

All you need to know about painting the metallic parts, such as chrome and aluminium, can be found in the painting chapter

at the beginning of this book, and all applies to this model. My experience with different metallic paints has revealed a common trait: all parts are sensitive to touch, working with them is demanding and any handling and manipulation can easily damage the delicate surface. Any finger grease creates 'maps' on the surface and dust particles can easily produce visible scratches. The aim is to manipulate the part after painting as little as possible. It is therefore essential to prepare everything related to component installation prior to painting. Quick installation is the only way to avoid part damage due to manipulation. Unfortunately, I was not precise enough in test-fitting and it caused me a headache while fitting the air cleaners, as well as the radiator grille and fuel tank. I even had to repaint some items. Ensuring well-painted metallic parts is just the

first half of the job, though, and you will only have succeeded after you have all the parts successfully installed on the model.

As for weathering, I did not want to apply much as all the vehicles in my references were clean. Oil paint washes and filters were applied all over the chassis and engine, while fine splatters of light mud over the mudflaps and chassis were created via the speckling method, and some grey and buff-toned oil paints, but that was all. Quick and simple this time.

CONCLUSION

My Pete 359 was built previously so, at the beginning, I thought this would be just a quick re-painting job, but it ended up with converted fenders, hood and hinges in attempt to correct some of the major geometrical errors – and with a completely new engine new fuel tank, battery box and wheels/tyes. The 359 is a true classic and it has all an American truck should have in terms of polished aluminium and chrome. Painting all the shiny bits requires both time and care, but once done properly it makes the model visually attractive and authentic. ■

11 *General Motors Company* CANNONBALL

This cab originally started life as a project for a double-drive long wheelbase truck with a 'Drom Box' body and an AMT Fruehauf van. I never managed to finish it and the stories of both the trailer and chassis are described elsewhere in this book. The moment the project was discarded the cab itself was in an advanced stage. It was well painted and had decent detail. It did not take much thought to realise it could be suitably employed on another chassis, making a good-looking 1950s single drive axle truck.

11.1 THE CAB

I got the cab as a simple resin conversion set, two friends of mine converted from a diecast model and fitted with a sleeper. I immediately fell in love with the rotund design of the vehicle widely known as Cannonball, named after a late 1950s TV series. Some cleaning was required on the cab and I finally reworked all the panel lines with a razor saw. The interior was fairly spartan, so I only used the resin dashboard and made a new floor from plastic sheet. I also found some seats in my spares box, along with a steering wheel. The sleeper was basically a flat box with holes where windows should be. I added some window rubbers made from Evergreen strip – which sounds like a quick job, but it was rather laborious as all the windows had rounded corners and I even abandoned the project for some time, just because of that. All the windows were cut out of clear plastic sheet and again, loads of curves made this a time-consuming task. For a better window fit, the cab shell wall thickness was reduced with a hand grinder. The original grille was replaced with a scratch-built item fitted with a CTM radiator front, from that company's White Freightliner set.

The vehicle livery was inspired by two old photos of various vehicles operated by the Mrazek moving company from St Louis, and all the decals were drawn by Jan Moštek and printed by decalprint.de, except for some scrolls and pinstripes I took from a KFS decal sheet. The cab was primed with Mr.Surfacer 1200, followed by gloss red Tamiya acrylic on the cab and sleeper and black on the hood,

TECH SPEC
GMC Cannonball

Kit: A limited resin kit by Jan Mostek and Jiri Hübner
Scale: 1:25
Accessories: KFS Spyder wheels, CTM 24127 Weld lines, CTM 24118 Semi truck tail lights, KFS air valve set
Notes: Decals drawn by Jan Mostek and printed by decalprint.de

fenders and front bumper. Applying the decals was easy, but numerous layers of a Tamiya gloss acrylic lacquer were needed to seal them. I originally meant to build a neat and shiny vehicle, but later the cab was sprayed with a satin clear coat, as this was more suitable for weathering.

Although sprayed already I found the sleeper walls too flat and boring. I received some CTM rivet decal sheets for pre-production testing and these were therefore added. They proved to be quite an easy and efficient way of enhancing the surface details of classic US trucks, but at the same time they were

quite fine and needed a precise paint job to be a real improvement. The problem with rivets in general, is that on many cabs they can easily get damaged during filling/sanding and reworking them is tricky. Gluing one after another using either resin rivets or plastic pads is difficult, time consuming and needs plenty of patience and care. Using a drill for making shallow holes instead of positive rivets is not very accurate either. The 'decal' rivets are basically thick blobs of paint added to decal backing, creating a sort of three-dimensional subject. Once applied the rivets may be sprayed over as they come in silver; however,

a heavy layer of paint on top can cause the rivets to disappear. While I quite liked the effect, but another modeller who had these for testing wasn't so enthusiastic, and CTM never put them into production. I do believe that Archer transfers has a similar product available though.

Once the sleeper was ready it was enclosed with a floor plate and attached to the cab. The cab's windows were fixed in place, being secured with water-based white glue. The dashboard was installed into the cab as well, and the floor with seats was inserted. The GMC letters on the grille were treated with

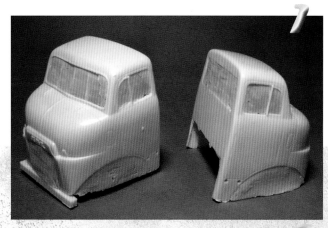

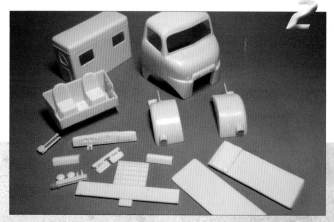

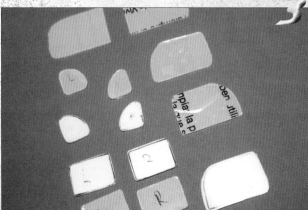

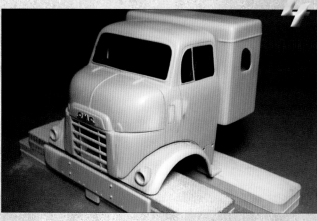

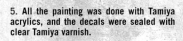

5. All the painting was done with Tamiya acrylics, and the decals were sealed with clear Tamiya varnish.

1. Typical for resin kits is that they come with flash and casting gates. This is normal and some careful cleaning may be required in the beginning.

2. The GMC kit wasn't much more than a cab shell with a bath tub style interior and a very few basic parts.

3. Resin kits come usually without windows. Plastic stencils were created and then the windows could be cut from a clear styrene sheet.

4. The cab needed a bit of work to improve the panel lines but once I had it in primer I fell in love with the look of it.

chromed Bare Metal Foil. The mirrors came from my spares box (Italeri DAF NTT) and the roof marker lights were left over from my Peterbilt 350 project, so I only sprayed them with Mr.Color Gloss Black followed by Alclad II Chrome. The original resin kit came with head lights, which I did not like, so I ground away the original lenses to provide thin frames, which I embellished with some old Scala43 lenses.

11.2 FRAME AND CHASSIS

In contrast to the original vehicle layout (a long wheelbase and a double drive), I finally opted for a short wheelbase single drive tractor. The period images show various GMC tractors in this configuration with different sleepers, exhaust and fuel tank options. I therefore felt relatively free about what components I could use on the chassis. My intention was to add as much detail to the frame as possible, but also to keep things quick and easy by using parts from my spares box. The basic feature of every model is a frame, but I did not have a suitable donor kit for building this subject and even if I had one, I would probably end up with scratch building my own frame as I simply like to have frame rails clean, smooth and made of thin material. The cab previously sat on a CNC-milled frame purchased from KFS. As the chassis dimensions worked perfectly, I built my own frame rails in the same height and width using 1mm sheet for the vertical rail section and Evergreen 0.75 x 4mm strips for the horizontal lengths. As the frame rails were of the same size as the original KFS parts, I was able to use some of the excess cross members from the spares box. All were modified and filled/sanded just like the outer frame rail surfaces. While the plastic cross members added the required rigidity to the frame, the photo-etched versions I had from testing some CTM prototype parts were employed to enhance the detail. The robust cross member right in front of the fifth wheel came from the CTM 035 MP4 Actros detail set, while the smaller item towards the front was from the CTM 24077 International chassis parts package.

Building frames always requires bolts and rivets to be added. There are different ways to go and each has its pros and cons. The resin rivets, nuts and bolts mostly offer better detail for a higher price and more difficult assembly, as only Superglue (and not standard modelling cement) can be used on them. On the other hand, the plastic nuts and bolts you can make yourself – either by cutting a round or hexagonal profile into the individual pads, or using a punch-and-die set with a piece of

1. There are several decal rivets available for cabs. These were the prototypes by CTM but Archer Transfers is well known for theirs too (sheets No 88033 and 88034 are suitable for our needs).

2. The rivets were treated like other decals. I used both the setter and softner with them.

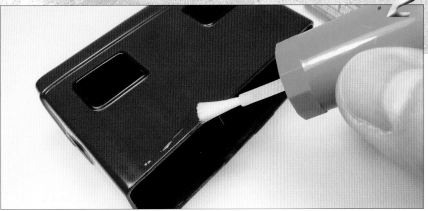

plastic sheet – are relatively cheap and allow the use of liquid cement for styrene. But the detail isn't usually that good. Recently, Meng has released a few sets with bolts and rivets that come on a plastic sheet, and all you need to do is cut them out and use them. Moulded in plastic, these somehow combine the advantages of both groups. I use all possible options on my models to stay away from any pattern, so I combine both plastic and resin for bolts and rivets, and I usually place the more expensive resin details where they will be more visible. The smaller photo-etched cross member, the top of the larger, and the related areas on the frame rails were detai-

led with resin rivet heads cut from the tree, and glued one after another to the metal parts using black Superglue. The rest of the frame was detailed with rivets made with a punch-and-die set that, which cuts the part from a piece of plastic sheet. I have sets for making both rounded and hexagonal pads, and often combine them for replicating various nuts and pad combinations or for plumbing fittings.

The front axle is a beautiful white metal casting from KFS, which did not need any modification. It was rigid enough to carry any weight of the resin cab and other accessories, and precise enough to prevent any 'pigeon-toed' wheel alignment. The front axle suspension

was a left-over from a Moebius International Prostar kit and was nearly a perfect fit for my model. However, the drive axle is a resin part I got from a friend and the springs originally came from Heller's Scania 141 kit. Both axles were fitted with resin hubs and KFS spider wheels. While the front tyres were standard Italeri parts, those for the rear were sourced from a 1/24 diecast kit.

I originally meant to use a pair of rounded fuel tanks on the model, but a pair of tanks from Italeri's Renault R360 fitted perfectly underneath the sleeper. I enclosed both tank ends with plastic sheet and added photo-etched weld lines from CTM's set 24127.

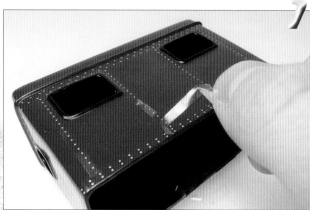

1. The CTM prototypes had the rivets under the film. Once dry, the film was to be removed and the rivets remained on the cab.

2. The rivets came in silver and for other cab colours they needed painting.

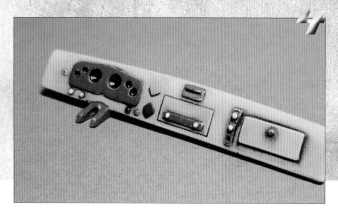

3. Very fine painting ensured that the rivet detail was not lost under the paint, which can easily happen with this pre-production rivet set.

4. The kit dashboard was simple but had sufficient detail and only needed careful brush painting.

5. Seats were made with a paper tissue and a cotton wool.

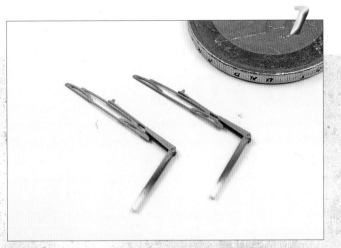

1. The photo etched wipers came from my spares box and were probably from a CTM set.

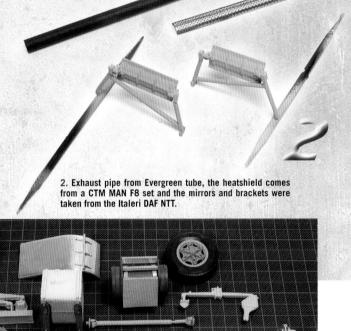

2. Exhaust pipe from Evergreen tube, the heatshield comes from a CTM MAN F8 set and the mirrors and brackets were taken from the Italeri DAF NTT.

The tank lids and data plates again were from the CTM White Freightliner bundle and all other surface details, including the straps, were removed to replicate the old 1950s tank style. The toolbox on the chassis is a full photo-etched item from the CTM 034 Peterbilt detail set, as well as the mud flaps with mounts; just the letters came from a PE set made for the GMC Astro. As the cab was not to tilt, and I did not want to have any of the access door open, only a dummy engine was used together with a transmission – both coming from an old KW K100 kit. The prop shaft was plundered from an old Italeri Volvo and was only cut to fit between the transmission and drive axle. All the air tanks and the fifth wheel are spares box items. The tail lights (although much newer in style than 195s') are the CTM 24119 items, which come with beautiful painted lenses and resin mounts. Revell's T600 provided the drive axle mudguards and these were cut to match the single drive arrangement.

Building the chassis was quick, so I had enough time to add regular plumbing. The basic parts were my usually favoured KFS white metal air valves. As they miss some appropriately sized outlets, I made my own fittings from various resin bolts. Four of the valves were enough for detailing the rear chassis end, and I placed them along the rails and on cross members. For the direct connection to the axles, rubber hoses were used on both the brake lines and the differential lock. The rest of the pipework was fashioned from copper wire. Each of the pipes was carefully bent to fit inside the frame and connect two points, and then fixed with in with Superglue. I always make sure the straight sections are perfectly straight, and the corners sharp and regular, so the result looks just like the real thing. In comparison to soft vinyl, working with copper wire

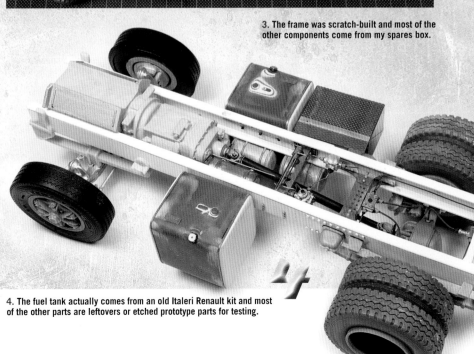

3. The frame was scratch-built and most of the other components come from my spares box.

4. The fuel tank actually comes from an old Italeri Renault kit and most of the other parts are leftovers or etched prototype parts for testing.

TECH-TIP:
HAIRSPRAY CHIPPING

Compared with the traditional hand-painting of chips, hairspray chipping is a completely different technique leading to the same thing – chipped paint. The principle is that you apply the rust colour first. Then follows a layer of hairspray and over that goes a layer of the final paint. Once you apply water and the hairspray starts dissolving, it is quite easy to remove the top paint layer either with a brush or an array of other tools such as a scalpel blade, a pin or toothpick. It may sound easy, however, success depends on a good combination of the thickness of the hairspray layer and the thickness and type of the top paint. The thinner the hairspray layer, the harder it is to remove the top paint. The thicker the layer of top paint, the harder it is for the water to reach the hairspray.

1 The hairspray chipping always starts with the basic layer. Its colour tone depends on the colour that follows. The lighter the colour, the darker the basic rust, the darker the colour, the lighter the rust.

2 There are different chipping mediums but I have worked with a regular hairspray in the past too and most of them can be used after some testing. The layer of hair spray comes in between for a good reason because it separates the two paint layers and reduces the adhesion of the upper layer so that it can be physically removed away after moistening the surface with water.

3 Once the hairspray is dry, the whole assembly can be sprayed with the final colour. Be easy on the airbrush trigger as the heavier the paint coat is, the harder the chipping. Avoid flooding the surface as the water based paint may react with the hairspray and ruin the result. Obviously, the upper paint coat must let the water to the hair spray underneath and melt it which means some type of paints are more suitable for this technique than the other ones. Water based acrylic paints are suitable for this method but some lacquer type paints work as well.

4 Once the paint is dry, the first step is to make the surface wet. This step is about moistening the parts and letting the water get underneath the paint and start dissolving the hairspray slowly.

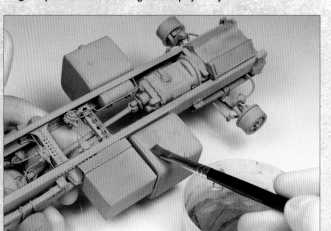

5 Allowing the water to get to the hair spray may take a few minutes. You can speed up the process by disturbing the paint layer on sharp edges or creating scratches on the exposed flat areas.

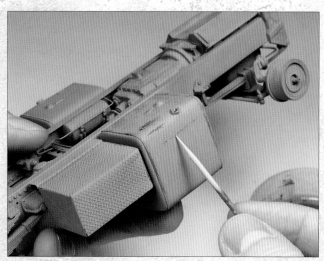

6 I use all types of brushes. The soft flat one works nicely on structured surfaces such as treadplates.

7 I use a flat brush with tough hair for a more aggresive approach when the paint has to be chipped harder.

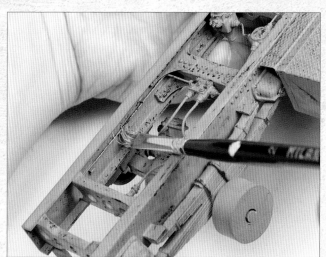

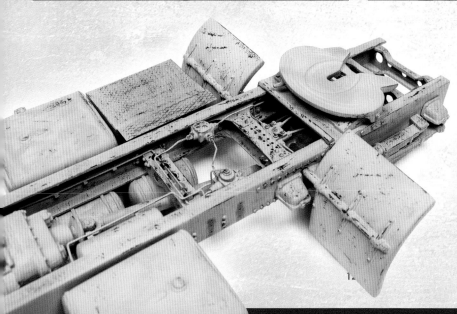

DONE!

Once the chips or scratches have been created the next step is to enhance their depth and colour with oils or acrylics. I usually go over the chips with oil paints, adding more colour tones inside as well as outside of the chipped areas mostly in terms of rust streaks as the rust particles are washed outside of the chipped areas.

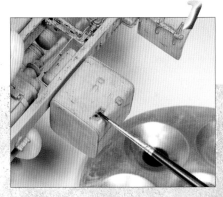

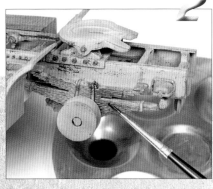

1. After the chipping and oil paint rendering, filters and washes followed.

2. The leaf springs always need a black or dark brown wash to highlight the gaps between the individual springs.

3. Dust and dirt were pre-sprayed on the tyres with Mission Models Tire black.

4. The rims were sprayed with hairspray, followed by the paint - ready for chipping.

5. Most of the chipping was done with a hard brush penetrating the paint on the sharp edges.

6. The beige rim edges stand out nicely on the grey chassis. A typical custom detail often seen on 50s trucks back then.

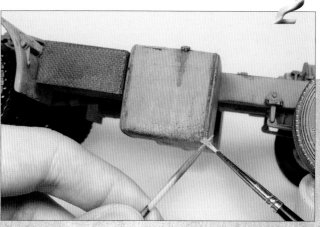

1. "What if there was toolbox or an air tank installed in this location previously?" I said to myself and painted two rusty rectangles as if a pair of mounts were removed from there recently.

2. Speckling was used to create splashes in the driving direction.

3. More pigments and oils were used on the splashes to make the result more random. Note that there is no rust oil paint applied to the chips yet.

is more time consuming and needs much patience, but it is the extra time that always gives your model an additional level of detail and a purposeful look.

Together with the photo-etched cross members, bolts and rivets, the wiring really boosted the authenticity – a far cry standard plastic kits. Given the fact that most of the components were leftovers from other kits, and that I didn't go crazy with the realism, all the work was very enjoyable.

11.3 PAINTING AND WEATHERING

Given the fact that the cab was painted during the pre-shelf queen model stage, I only had to add colour to the chassis. Weathering had to be done for both. I am quite conservative in terms of which shades I use for both painting and weathering, and once I find a reliable method, I seldom step away from it. I therefore choose mostly Mr.Color and Tamiya acrylics because they provide a complete system, from primer to decal solvents. However, I made broke from the norm on the GMC chas-

sis as I had received some test sample acrylics from a newly established brand and I decided to try them, as you never learn anything new if you don't step outside of your comfort zone. The paint samples were from the recently introduced Mission Models range, which came together with grey primer, thinner and a polyurethane mix additive for improving the paint spraying performance and finish.

As a big fan of Mr.Surfacer, I was curious to know if the Mission Models primer would perform anywhere as well, so I diluted it as per the instructions (30% thinner) and started spraying the chassis. With the engine, transmission, axles and fuel tanks fitted this was a pretty complex assembly, and it took time and patience to get the primer into all the corners, but I must admit it performed quite well and the sprayed surface was pleasingly smooth. I didn't use any of the additive, but it would have made the result even better.

As hairspray chipping was meant to be the main process for the chassis weathering, I sprayed the chassis with my favourite mixture of Mr.Finishing Surfacer Black and Mr.Color Hull Red 29 I use for the basic dark rust colour, followed by Worn Effects from AK Interactive. I applied a generous layer and let it dry. The topcoat is a fine layer of Mission Models RAL 7016 Grey, sprayed with a hint of the ori-

The frame and cab ready for marriage before the final weathering stages.

ginal thinner. After some models I've finished using the hairspray method, I feel comfortable with it and find it very effective. While hand painting chips on the Volvo F12 frame shown in another chapter took countless hours, chipping the GMC frame was done in one evening. The method itself is described elsewhere in this book and what I did on the GMC is exactly the same. The first step is always to apply a small amount of water on the area you want to chip. The water slowly dissolves the chipping liquid (hairspray) underneath – depending on the top coat opacity – and lets you pick up

your tool (a brush, toothpick or anything you find suitable to use) and start chipping the top coat from the surface to reveal the base coat underneath. I always combine different types of tool to achieve various effects: brushes for random chips and edges and various sharp tools for long, thin scratches.

After chipping the oil paints, always follow in the form of filters, washes or more artistic oil paint rendering. I used a black wash for all the surface details, bolts, leaf springs and welds and later focused on smaller areas, carrying out more rendering using the chips

and surface details as a guide where some rust streaks would occur, and where grease and dirt would collect. I did not use any pigments – but relied on the speckling method to add small mud and dirt splashes around the wheels, and all lower chassis areas. Speckling is fun to do and is relatively quick. With basic practice you can achieve realistic results. Just focus on having it all in scale and in the right place. The rims were chipped with the hairspray technique and treaded with oils, just like the frame.

The cab also received filters after the panel

1. A black oil paint wash was used to highlight all the panel lines. I always use a fine pointed brush that makes it easy to delivery the wash into the recessed detail.

2. The chips on the cab were painted in two layers. The first layer was done in a bright pinkish tone on the cab and sleeper.

3. To replicate the chips that went through the paint down to the metal I added another layer, painting dark brown into the centre of the bright chips.

4. I like to enhance the rusty chips and scratches with rust tone oil paints. It usually means delivering a small drop of paint into the centre of the chip and fading it with a little bit of thinner to make the edge rather soft.

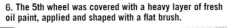

6. The 5th wheel was covered with a heavy layer of fresh oil paint, applied and shaped with a flat brush.

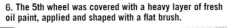

5. The same style of chips was painted on the hood but in grey for a visible contrast. Not all the chips have to turn into rust.

General Motors Company Cannonball

lines were highlighted with a dark wash. A light dust oil paint was applied in the form of vertical streaks, carefully blended to create soft effects. Some chips were painted in a sort of pinkish colour (on red) and grey (on black), with additional dark brown chips in the centre to represent the exposed rusty metal underneath. These chips were again enhanced with rust-coloured oil paints. The dirt on windows was replicated with stencils and buff oil paint, in the same way as described elsewhere in this guide..

CONCLUSION

It is always fun to sit down once you finish a model, look around and think whether finishing something old wouldn't be a better alternative rather than starting something new. This was the exact case of my GMC and not only that I have made use of the cab that was in a good shape already, but I also used many of the various spares box items that looked useless but altogether they made a great model almost for free. No matter how you get it (whether you bought a bunch of older models built by someone else, collect the leftovers from all the kits you built before or scrap your own work after time) a box of spare parts and various model components, cabs, wheels and engines will always broaden your horizon during building and converting your model. It often saves time that you would normally spend with scratch building of what you need. Some of the parts can be easily used over and over to save your time and energy when you want to speed up the building process and have fun with how the model grows in your hands quickly. ■

12 VOLVO F12

I like classics. Their style interests me and I also love the technology hidden inside them. So if it comes from between the 1950s-1980s (and from either side of the Atlantic ocean) I like to dig deep into the brochures, manuals and all the literature I come across to find more about the engines, transmissions, suspension systems and so on.

12.1 INTRODUCTION

Some of those trucks I know well enough to perform the real vehicle maintenance straight away. The Volvo F12 is one such example, and each time I build one it's really a special occasion. With the knowledge of the full-size vehicle comes an idea of what each individual kit component should look like; it is therefore quite difficult to incorporate any shortcuts into the project. In fact, it took about

five years and three attempts to finish building this model. The model's livery changed a few times from something fictional over PKS and Hungarocamion to Den Hartogh and finally PKS again, as I wanted to have one of the Polish trucks in my collection. The PKS F12 tractors were kept rather simple with absolutely no accessories – the wildest creation being a different colour of cab corner deflector, so there was not much to choose from.

All truck modellers know Italeri's kit

No.751. It was the first 1/24 scale model kit (and first truck) from that company back in 1981, and it has appeared in many different forms since then. The kit is good and accurate, but also simply a product of its time, with the associated pitfalls. It's relatively simple, which is not a problem, but in my eyes the engine and transmission are far too basic, with many components moulded on the one engine block instead of providing separate detailed parts. The way the engine is fashio-

TECH SPEC
Volvo F12

Kit: 751 Italeri VOLVO F12
Scale: 1:24
Accessories: CTM 001 Volvo F12 details set, CTM 24086 Volvo F12 lights, CTM 24121 Volvo F16 (tail) lights, KFS split rims, KFS new resin air valves, KFS Cab junk set, my own resin engine and transmission
Notes: Decals drawn by Karel Vaclavík, printed by decalprint.de

ned makes any detailing difficult, as even the exhaust manifold is just a part of the engine head, so there are no clearances where the injection pipes should be routed, and so on.

12.2 ENGINE

Using the engine from the kit was not an option. I got too close to the real old Volvo trucks to be able to build this out of the box, so I decided to cut both the 1/24 Italeri and 1/25 Revell powerplants into pieces and combine them. It needed a good portion of scratch building and converting too. As I plan to build

more old Volvos in the future, I had the engine cast and was pleased with the interest shown by other modellers. Once I had the resin parts from the caster, it just needed assembling and detailing with the basic fuel and air lines to get it ready for painting. It sounds easy, but in reality, the whole process took about a year.

Painting and weathering engines has been described in a detailed chapter elsewhere in this book. What I did on this Volvo is well within the usual process and techniques. I opted for hand painted chipping this time, so the basic coat is my own green mixed from different Mr.

Color paints diluted with that firm's Leveling Thinner. I did not bother with the particular tone too much, as in the next step I played with the look via light oil paint filters to get the desired appearance. Regarding engines, it is easiest for me to assemble them completely and then hand paint the details afterwards, so all the accessories, wiring and exhaust were accentuated with Vallejo acrylics after the filtering stage.

I favour both the hairspray technique and hand painted chipping – and try to keep reasonably well practised with both, so for the

1. The original engine vs. my own resin version. It has all the components separate and loads of details added.

2. The resin engine was so detailed that it only needed fuel lines to look perfect, although they required some patience and care.

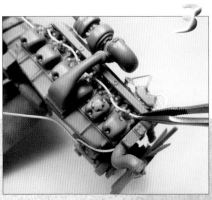

3. While the high pressure fuel lines are steel pipes, the overflow hose is soft and the difference should be clearly visile on the model.

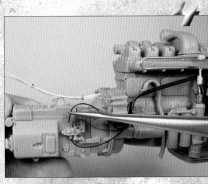

4. There is a splitter control valve located on the transmission side which got some air lines added.

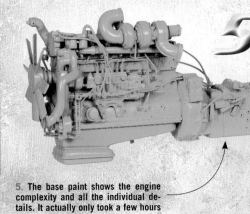

5. The base paint shows the engine complexity and all the individual details. It actually only took a few hours to assemble.

Volvo engine I decided to hand paint all the chips, and follow quickly with oil paint rendering for rust, local wash and dirt effects. The PKS truck was meant to represent a working vehicle in its prime, so I was aiming just for a modicum of operational damage rather than any heavy rust. What I wanted to show, however, was intense paint chipping on the aluminium components such as the injection pump, flywheel housing, inlet manifold or rocker covers. All this was hand painted with Agama Aluminium and significantly enhanced with white and light grey oil paint. Small fresh green chips were then painted around the large exposed surfaces. I had useful reference photos for the exhaust manifold and turbocharger, showing the authentic colour tones perfectly, with the purplish turbine housing and manifold and a brighter engine brake housing. Some of the darker rust spots were hand painted, the finer examples being replicated by speckling. Both acrylics and oils were combined here.

Most of the engine dirt represents prolonged, slow oil leakage into which dust and dirt is trapped, creating dark stains all around the engine, especially in its lower areas. I could have pushed the trigger harder in some areas

but, again, just a regularly maintained working truck was desired.

The finished engine was then ready for attachment to the chassis; the exhaust outlet and gearstick mount and linkage were added during the final assembly as adjustment was needed.

12.3 CHASSIS

While the engine is a heavily modified resin version of the original, the rest of the chassis is quite close to what can be found in the kit. Apart from a shorter wheelbase, I did not feel the need for any greater modifications and

1. The KFS air valves, both the older white metal and new resin ones, are an absolute must for any frame detailing and wiring.

2. Plastruct hexagon rods, black insulated wire, black fishing nylon, black heat shrink tubing, copper wire in different diameters, CTM cable ties and resin fittings is what I use for the plumbing and wiring.

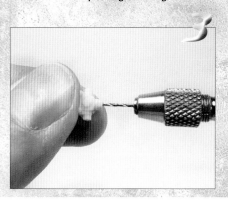

3. For easier wire installation I always drill holes into all the valves and fittings. It makes the whole wiring operation a lot quicker.

4. The whole model was built and detailed first, and only after that all the components were primed with Mr.Surfacer.

TECH-TIP: ENGINE WEATHERING

Weathering engines does not demand any specific technique. It is a combination of all the methods on a specific subject – filters, washes, oil paint rendering, rust... you name it. One common thing to all my engines is that I always try to add as many details as possible before painting, and to paint and weather it all as one entire complex part. Just as I hand-paint all the details, I also weather the whole assembly one area after another. In general, the process is: painting the engine (airbrushing, colour modulation, HS technique), hand-painted details (components, rubber hose, etc), washes and filters, hand-painted chips, exhaust rust, OPR, oil leaks and rust.

1 First, a light dust filter was applied in several layers to tone the bright green down and match the engine with the weathered chassis.

2 All the details were brush painted. I always assemble the engine completely before painting it. For me it is an easier way to keep everything clean and avoid any traces of glue.

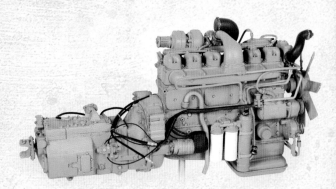

3 Next step, once all the details were hand painted, was a black oil paint wash. Note the added contrast and depth around all the surface details, bolts, covers and gaps.

4 Aluminium chips were painted all over the aluminium components with Agama silver metal paint. Note that oil paint rendering was also done on this side, especially the heavy leakage on the oil sump.

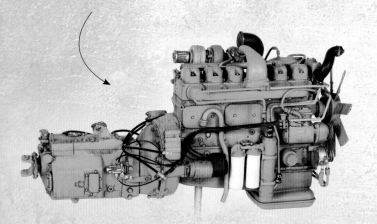

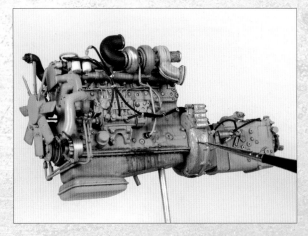

5 Fine chips were painted all over the steel casting, using Vallejo acrylics. Note that some of the chips have bright edges that were painted before the dark rust ones were added.

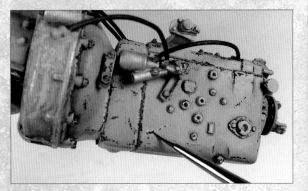

6 Most of the chips were enhanced with rust oil paints during the next round of oil paint rendering.

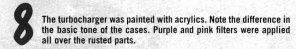

7 More oil leaks were painted around the covers on the right hand side of the engine. All with a fine brush and a black oil paint.

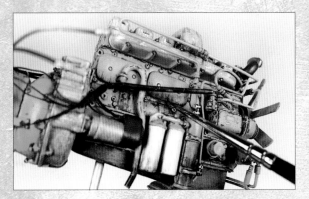

8 The turbocharger was painted with acrylics. Note the difference in the basic tone of the cases. Purple and pink filters were applied all over the rusted parts.

9 Next step of the rust painting was to add small irregular dots that are typical for exhaust manifolds and turbochargers. (see page 38)

10 The most delicate spots were made with the speckling method using a fine brush for a precise and controlled application.

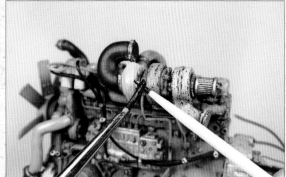

DONE!

The engine weathering consists of many layers. Note for example that additional dark oils were added over the oil sump. This process is here shown in just a few pictures but it means many more layers, drying time, additional layers and building all the effects slowly and with full control. Do not expect to do this in one evening session. This particular engine took about a month with an hour or two spent on it every day.

tings made from Plastruct hexagon rods and resin elbow fittings. These come from a set I haven't been able to find again, so once I ran out of those in a proper size during this build, I made my own from a piece of wire and hex rods, and used them on the air tanks. The engine fitted into the chassis perfectly, as both were continuously test-fitted prior to any painting.

The frame was primed and sprayed with Mr.Color 327 Gloss Red. It gave a superb fine and lustrous surface, but in hindsight I should have used satin varnish over that, which would have helped with the oil paints' adhesion. Once red the chassis was masked, the black fender tops and battery box cover were sprayed flat black. The fuel tank was painted separately as it was in natural aluminium; I used Mr.Color Silver No.8 first and then the tank straps were masked and sprayed red. Frame weathering started with a black oil paint wash applied around the bolt heads, over the springs, wheel hubs and into the corners. Red-orange filters were used on the frame as I wanted to avoid shifting the tone towards pink. Dark green was added to the black components. Hand painting chips on this model took considerable time as the 1/24 frame is large and has many delicate compo-

just small details were changed. The cab's coiled springs were made from a piece of wire which replaced the unrealistic plastic part. The frame and axles received bolts and nuts all around, some of which where plastic, while others were resin. I embellished the air tanks with CTM 24189 air tank data plates, and the CTM 001 Volvo F12 set was also useful for the chassis, which received the spare wheel

carrier, fuel tank straps and a catwalk. The wheel hubs were a resin item and the rims are the classic KFS Split rim wheels employed by Polish F12s. The way I replicate wiring on my models is well known. A must have are KFS air valves (for this model I purchased the firm's latest resin examples, which are beautifully detailed) as well as CTM cable ties. I also used cables and copper wires, hexagonal fit-

1. The frame was sprayed with Mr.Color red, no. 327. I usually spray the frames as one large assembly, as I think that is the smoothest way.

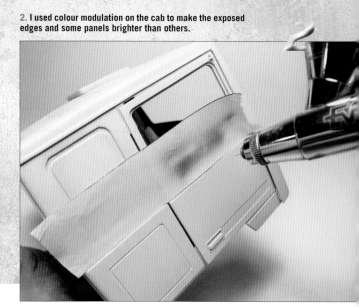

2. I used colour modulation on the cab to make the exposed edges and some panels brighter than others.

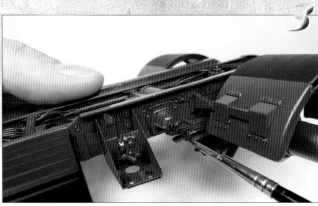

3. Oil paint filters and washes were applied all over the frame.

nents. It was nowhere close to the effectivity of the hair spray technique used on the GMC Cannonball, but it was good to see what the differences might be. I made my own wet palette and used Vallejo acrylics applied with fine new brushes. The chips were meant to be small – just the early variety that appear on the edges of steel components – or those that come from everyday wear and tear.

On the other hand, the amount of dust and dirt was mean to be relatively high, as I wanted a vehicle that had arrived from a long journey on dirty European roads in autumn. I started with dark grey oil paint applied all around the frame rails, providing the oldest and darkest dirt, a mixture of grease and brake lining dust and road dirt accumulated over the vehicle. This was followed by brighter dry mud spatters made with both the oils and pigments, emulating a vehicle that had to negotiate a short muddy road or a yard for loading or unloading.

Being made of aluminium, the fuel tank haves quite specifically were not cleaned and polished regularly. The aluminium loses its lustre relatively quickly, and the aggressive environment of grease, salt and rough winter conditions create maps and dots on the surface that only encourage more dirt. I started with generic filter layers to obtain basic surface variation. On this, very fine vertical streaks were replicated with buff oil paint, hand painted, and followed by more thin oil filters and oil

1. The surface after wash and multiple orange filters and ready for chipping.

2. In contrast to the GMC frame, all the chips were brush painted with Vallejo acrylics and the whole process took many hours.

3. This is the end result of the chipping. I always focus on the smallest chips first and only carefully add the larger ones to keep the result balanced. The picture above provides an interesting comparison.

4. The chips usually form on sharp edges first and so I painted them all along the frame rail edges, air tank traps and so on. Note that there are only small chips as the vehicle is still relatively new.

5. Many of the cab parts were made from fibreglass, hence the white chips on the deflectors and mudguards. Many vehicles have specific areas prone to rust and in case of the F series Volvos it has been the lower cab side areas and the toolbox door.

6. This pair of pictures clearly shows the difference between the fresh brush painted chips and what oil paint rendering does to the area. Note the wash in the panel lines, rust around the chips and dust on the wheelarch.

TECH-TIP: DUST WITH OILS/PIGMENT

Using oil paints and pigments for creating dust and dirt is a classic approach. There is no exact guide how the weathering should be done and how the techniques should follow. The key is in applying fine layers and building the effects gently, working smaller areas in detail. Add dust and dirt where it tends to collect, make splatters, add rust tones on the exposed edges and chipped paint areas, paint streaks on vertical surfaces, fuel stains around the fuel tank filling cap, oil leaks around the engine, transmission and drive axles and wash to highlight all the details.

1 Once the filters and washes were dry I started with layering the dirt. The first one was a contrasting dark grey.

2 Next was the light dust and buff tones in multiple layers followed by speckling.

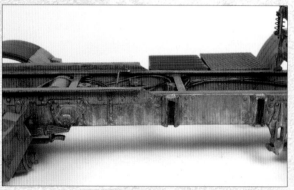

3 Horizontal surfaces inside the frame are typical for collecting layers of dirt. Pigments were used for this.

4 The speckling method is very useful for creating random splashes of dirt as seen on the mudflaps here.

5 Making the vehicle dirty on the outside and leaving it clean inside is an easy mistake that many modellers make. Painting in sub assemblies makes the weathering process easier.

6 The stains on the fuel tank were made with dust filters, fine speckling spots and then finally carefully painted streaks and fuel stains.

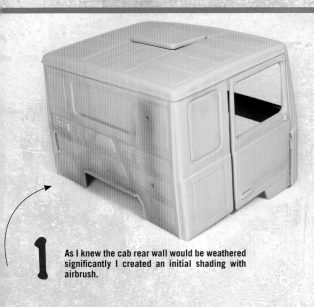

1 As I knew the cab rear wall would be weathered significantly I created an initial shading with airbrush.

2 On the cab, a little darker mud was used for a better contrast on the bright yellow. The oil paint was applied with speckling and then blended vertically with a brush. This was repeated a few times with different colours for a more interesting result.

3 The pre-shaded areas provide a foundation when building darker and heavier layers of older dirt typical for rear cab walls on trucks.

4 The cab bottom and mudguards are rarely properly cleaned on trucks. These should therefore carry layers of dirt collected over the years.

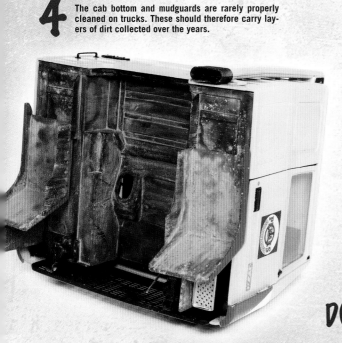

DONE!

paint rendering. Speckling was used to create the finest dark dots as well as the dirt splatters from the wheels.

12.4 THE CAB

The cab wasn't modified too much either, as what comes in the kit is generally good. The CTM detail set did its job on the grille, but there was not much space for other detailing on the painted dashboard panels, as what

the model needs the kit already has – little else being necessary. I bought the kit quite a long time ago, partially built, because none of the re-issues were available at the time. The original kit owner did a great job, and what was assembled and glued was done cleanly. I couldn't have done it any better and I was happy it saved me time. What the man also did well was that he hinged the door using a piece of wire and thin brass sheet. I am not a

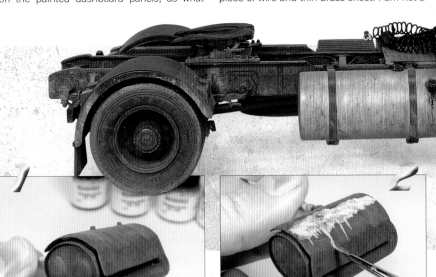

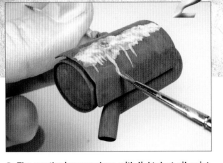

1. The basic rust on the exhaust was painted with Lifecolor acrylics just like shown on the PIE Peterbilt exhaust earlier.

2. The weathering was done with light dust oil paint. First the rough streaks were applied and then blended with a flat brush and a minimal amount of thinner.

4. The gearstick linkage was all scratchbuilt since it was missing completely in the kit.

3. The finished exhaust with two layers of oil paints and pigments dust applied on the wet surface with speckling.

5. The interior was built as per instructions and painted in the original colours. Long distance trucks have a lots of cab accessories and I always enjoy detailing the interiors with everyday items.

big fan of working features on truck models as they usually encourage damage, but this worked good enough, so I left the hinge as it was. However, door and cab modifications were needed to reduce the gap around the door, and to create at least a basic door frame. The floor pan was busy with interior detail, but it suffered in that the bunk, dashboard and other areas were open from below. As the cab tilted, the floor pan bottom was visible, so all these areas were enclosed with plastic sheet. Other than that, the cab was built as per the instructions.

This book has a dedicated chapter on detailing interiors, dealing with everything invol-ved in detailing the Volvo cab. I like interiors busy, with everyday junk and drivers' belong-ings, but I must admit that any time I drive a truck I always ensure my cab is the exact opposite. I used flocking on the seats and bunk, but I think I will stay away from it for a few projects as I expected more from it – but was unable to get the exact results I wanted. Most of the interior add-ons are my own items, from all the paperwork, magazine and a pizza box to the spare parts collection in the passenger area. The travel bag and shoes are resin from KFS and the Coke bottle (also resin) was by PlusModel.

The cab was assembled in the usual way and all exterior weathering was conducted after its installation on the chassis. The roof and interior walls had to be added first, followed by the floor with dash. All windows were fixed in place with white glue, which I always use for glazing to prevent damage that is difficult to remedy. The cab steps came from CTM , s well as the wipers and headlights. These received some wiring as the bumper inner parts are pleasingly visible when the cab is up. The PKS decals and number plates were drawn by Karel Václavík.

Relatively simple colour modulation was employed when the cab shell was sprayed, to ensure basic colour variation in the bright yellow, especially along the horizontal edges on the side walls. Dark stains were added to the rear cab, under the air intake channel and along the lower edges, which always get dirty by hot air leaving the engine compartment and mixing with exhaust fumes, oil and dirt. The yellow colour is my own blend of Mr.Color paint and all I followed were period photos showing that the PKS yellow was really bright,

but that is the only thing I remember from mixing the paint. It is just a regular yellow with a hint of white added. Filter layers were also applied to the cab, mostly in buff and light dust shades.

I started weathering with hand painting white chips on the fenders and corner deflector, which are both plastic, and this type of wear is often evident on older vehicles. I did the same on the bumper parts, except for the light frames which are made of steel, so their chips were rendered in dark brown. The bumper lower part was made of aluminium and later weathered with oil paints and pigments. The main visual component of the yellow cab weathering is that of small rusty spots. It is well known that 1970s and 80s trucks mostly 'died' of corrosion rather than mechanical failure, and I wanted to use the bright cab to show that on the typical F12 areas, such as the lower cab edges and driver's side locker door. Once all the chips were painted, I went over all of them with dark brown oil paint, adding the typical soft rust transition to each. The next layer comprised dirt in multiple layers, using mostly oil paints applied by brush and blended vertically, as if washed down by rain.

CONCLUSION

Finishing this model brought much relief, as it was a successful end to a long journey. It gave me the chance to develop individual engine details that have made many modellers (and me) very happy – and that I will be able use in my future Volvo models effectively. With a PKS truck I added another classic from the Comecon countries to my collection, and I'm sure it won't be the last. ■

13 FERGUSON
TE-20

The little grey Ferguson TE-20 was a small agricultural tractor popular in Europe throughout the 20th century.

13.1 INTRODUCTION

There is quite a long story behind this vehicle, regarding the cooperation between Ferguson and Ford, due to which modified tractors were also produced under the Ford name in Detroit, Michigan and were popular in the US at the same time. Model kits of any agricultural vehicles are very rare, and apart from the vintage Ertl and AMT kits there was very little else until recently, when kits of small antique agricultural tractors started appearing on the market.

The Heller Ferguson was the first of them and it's brilliant in many ways. It is beautifully detailed so it can be built into a very accurate model without modification. And it is small, so it can be constructed quickly if you don't want to tackle anything complex with hundreds of parts, and there is less weathering area too. All these reasons made me build it, although agricultural equipment has never been my focus in modelling. The intense weathering and how well some techniques can be shown on it made me include the model in this book, despite the primary focus being on regular.

A great thing about the TE-20 is that it was available in medium grey. Once it fades to light grey, it is basically the best colour tone on which to portray chipping and rust effects. Yes, there are good and bad colours for weathering. Grey is ideal, while red is an extremely difficult canvas on which to create any rust. Since the very early building stage I knew how I wanted the model to look, most of the effects being rendered with the hairspray technique. I had useful reference photos taken years ago at Gaydon model truck festival in England, showing a well-worn but still maintained TE-20. These exemplified the difference between the aluminium and cast-iron components of the tractor and what I wanted

Kit: Ferguson TE-20
Scale: 1/24
Accessories: PE lights with milled aluminum frames, KFS numberplates, KFS tax disc decals
Notes: The grille gaps were cut through, the toolbox is made of a aluminum sheet, otherwise built from the box

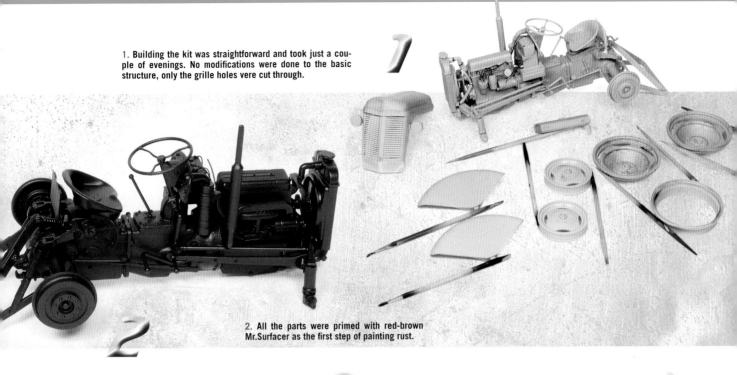

1. Building the kit was straightforward and took just a couple of evenings. No modifications were done to the basic structure, only the grille holes vere cut through.

2. All the parts were primed with red-brown Mr.Surfacer as the first step of painting rust.

3. The transmission case and some engine components were made of aluminum so they were painted differently.

4. Oil paint filters were used on the aluminum castings to create authentic weathered aluminum.

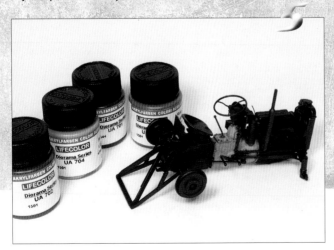

5. All the steel components were then painted with the Vallejo rust colour set.

6. The only little detail changed was a little toolbox scratchbuilt of aluminum sheet to replace the original one.

to show on my model. Assembly took just a couple of days and was in full accordance with the instructions, apart from adding distributor and spark plug wires, replaced the plastic toolbox with a new version made from aluminium sheet, and cutting the grille apertures with a razor saw. What took much longer was the painting.

13.2 COLOUR AND RUST

A mixture of Mr.Finishing Surfacer Black and a Mr.Color brown shade acted as a primer, applied over the Tamiya putty used to make

a rough casting structure. The transmission case was an aluminium casting, so I masked the engine and rear end with Tamiya tape and sprayed the gearbox light blue. Various dots of different sizes were applied over this, using a piece of sponge with dark blue and silver paint, and the whole area was filtered multiple times with white and light grey oil paints. Bolt heads and nuts were highlighted with brush-painted dark brown. A brush was also used to enliven the transfer case and engine, via a Lifecolor rust and dust set, one after another, to create random and authentic

bright rust effects. Black wash was applied around the details and oil paints altered the rust tones slightly, making them darker and more dramatic. I wanted the three-point hitch linkage to be fully exposed and therefore covered with old rust, which is typically very dark and has various tones, from dark brown to purple.

I started by applying darker tones from the Lifecolor set, using a piece of sponge and then followed with oil paint filters of black-brown and dark purple.

The whole front end was treated similarly, with the engine block in iron and the oil sump, rocker cover and radiator in aluminium. Again, oil paints were used to enhance the colour tones and black wash added contrast. Once dry, the whole assembly was sprayed with AK Interactive Worn Effects. The model was then chipped in three main sections, which were sprayed and chipped individually. Rather than a brush I used a sharp toothpick or a scalpel blade to remove the paint from edges and create scratches. The fuel tank, hood and wheels were painted separately, and the rear wheels received Lifecolor rust prior to the hairspray application; smaller parts such as the hood, mudguard and fuel tank had just the dark brown primer applied, which is good enough for smaller chips and scratches.

While one part of the success with hairspray is creating accurately sized and spaced chips, the second that follows is being able to use the potential of the hairspray technique and enhance the re-

TECH-TIP:
HEAVY RUST CHIPPING

In heavy chipping, both painting rust and hairspray chipping is combined. First the authentic rust-coloured surface is painted and then hairspray chipping is conducted, but with a much larger chipped area exposing significantly more of the rust surface than in the case of fine chips and scratches. The key to authentic rust is applying various colours in transparent layers. This leads to subtle colour variations of the basic surface and it does not matter whether you work with acrylic paints, oils or pigments. Of course, once the chipping is finished, another run of rust painting and adding more effects with oil paints is carried out.

1 Normally I just use a dark rust primer as a chipping background but with the tractor I knew I will be exposing a lot larger area than usual so I made a more detailed rust painting all over the iron parts using the Lifecolor acrylics.

2 The painted rust surface can be enhanced in many ways. One of them is using a piece of sponge for creating random rust spots.

3 Oil paints for washes, filters and individual rendering are another level of detailing the rust structure. Here dark wash is being applied around the details.

4 Note the parts of the three point hitch are much darger rust then the rest. This was done with purple and dark brown filters.

5 Before the chipping medium was applied, the whole model surface had a detailed paintjob done underneath including the weathered aluminium where required.

6 For heavier chipping the top coat layer has to be fine so that it is easier to remove it in larger portions.

7 The same model area after chipping. Note the completely different apperance of the model before and after the technique.

8 The tools for chipping are mostly different brush sizes. I use an old fine brush for a harder rubbing details.

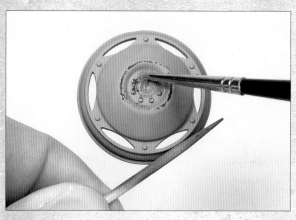

9 I use a fine hair flat brush for applying water and the initial long and fine chips on the exposed edges.

10 The oil paint rendering always starts with a cardboard palette for removing the excess oil from the paints.

11 One after another a small amount of oil paint is delivered in each chipped area and is blended with the surrounding surface.

1. The location and size of the chips matters. Sharp edges and exposed areas such as the side wall next to the brake pedal where drivers feet move frequently.

2. Oil paint rendering in practise: the chips provide a guide where the oils are applied. Not the difference comparing to the state fresh after chipping in the previous picture.

4. Using the oil paints a larger contrast between the chips and the outer surface can be reached.

3. Once the chips are created, the oil paint rendering comes into play. I use a fine pointed brush and a thinned oil paint for enhancing the rusty chips.

5. The dust over the mudguards was applied only in a very soft transparent layer.

6. Note that the final result is very fine and transparent. Weathering properly and under control means many soft layers rather than heavy single one.

sult with oil paints. That basically means going over each chip and scratch with a fine brush and rust-tone oils, creating streaks or just softening the rust edges, adjusting the contrast and so on. This was conducted all over the model including the hood, wheels and mudguards. Rust on the exhaust was once again painted with the Lifecolor set, but the brightest areas were rendered with skin tone oil paint.

13.3 DUST AND DIRT

The light dust on the inside of the mudguards is a buff-toned 502 Abteilung oil paint, while the outer side was covered with pigments blended with Odourless thinner and followed by speckling various AK Interactive enamel weathering products.

The most difficult to weather were the rear tyres as they are made of rubber and the witness mark is virtually impossible to remove. Not only that, the mud in the tread should look realistic but also needs to cover that. The pillow on the seat was made of Miliput, painted with Vallejo acrylics and weathered with oils. British number plates came from a KFS decal set as well as the tax permit on the engine cowling. The lights are photo-etched with a CNC milled frame and were offered some time ago by modelmakershop.

CONCLUSION

While building this subject was relatively quick, the painting took about a month and needed plenty of patience and care. I could afford to spend so much time on the individual components, purely because the model is small and relatively simple. I cannot imagine weathering every individual component of a 1/24 or 1/25 model truck that much in detail, simply because of their size and the time and concentration required. In my eyes, a smaller project is more suitable for tackling a challenging paint finish. ■

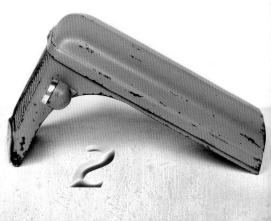

1. The position and amount of chips over the model surface has to be random. Even in the real life some areas suffer with corrosion more, some are almost intact with maybe some initial chips showing.

2. There is a ballance in what good looks on the model and how things are happening in the real world. The rust and chips do not occur in all places with the same intensity. While the drivetrain of this tractor was chipped heavily, there was no need to add any severe battle damage to the hood.

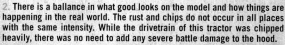

3. The exhaust rust was done with layering Vallejo acrylics in transparent coats.

TECH-TIP:
HEAVY DIRT AND MUD

Pigments are well-known weathering products. They come in various colours: different rust tones, all dust and mud, soil or sand colours, black for smoke effects and metal colours for painting metallic parts. Pigments can be applied both dry and wet and can be mixed. They need a matt surface underneath for decent adherence. A popular way of applying pigments is making thick layers to show heavy mud and dirt. The most common liquid for working with pigments are the usual thinners for working with oil paints and washes, such as white spirit or AK Interactive odourless thinner. When needed, pigments may be fixed on a model using dedicated fixer.

 Creating heavy pigment layers is fun and very easy. The firt step is to apply a dry layer of pigments. This can consist of different colours for more authentic effect.

 Once applied you slowly start fixing the pigments with thinner. Using a pigment fixer will help creating a more durable layer.

 To add intensity and colour variation, some additional speckling can be done with various enamel weathering products or oil paints.

 The finished effect after drying. The colour variation was achieved by using different nuances of pigments, enamels and oils.

DONE!
QUICK &
EASY

AND HERE'S HOW IT'S DONE ON A TRUCK CHASSIS!

1 A heavy dirt layer is typical for many off-road vehicles. It collects mostly around the wheels and on the lower chassis.

2 Once the dry pigment has been applied, add some thinner or fixer to attach the pigments to the surface properly.

3 Speckling of pigments and oil paints is great for adding another layer of random splashes of mud and dirt.

4 Wet mud areas in corners can be made with adding darker oil paints to the brighet pigments.

5 Don't forget to add oil leaks over the engine sump, transmission and axles. These rarely stay dry on older vehicles.

14 MERCEDES
1222 LF16

To be honest, I have never really been a fan of fire engines or tackling them as modelling subjects. Not for any particular reason, but they have just not attracted me in the same way as long haulers. Still, there are always exceptions to the rule, and this one managed to catch my attention.

14.1 INTRODUCTION

From all the fire engine kits available there is just one that 'grabbed' me the first time I saw it. That was well over 20 years ago, shown in a diorama in a Revell catalogue, and it was an old NG-series Mercedes-Benz double cab – the LF16. Most likely because of the double cab type otherwise usually available in scale, I fell in love with it. After many years of visiting the On the Road Model Show in Belgium I came across the original issue of the kit from 1987. The decals were missing, otherwise the kit was complete and for a fair price, so I just

bought it, happy that I had a kit for which I always had a weakness. That was just a couple of weeks after finishing my PKS Volvo F12 and right when I was searching for the last model to complete this book. On my way from Belgium I already knew the LF16 would be my last missing piece of the puzzle.

The kit itself is great even today. Being 30 years old the parts still look good, the detail is sharp, and it was not difficult to imagine that with just a couple of modifications it could make a pleasing model. The modifications summary is surprisingly short: the plastic tread plate on the roof and side steps

was replaced with photo-etched catwalk, the bumper was embellished with scratch-built headlight reflectors, the grille openings were cut through and one of the shutter doors was left open and its interior detailed. Apart from that the kit was built as per the instructions and nothing extra was added, except for some photo-etched 'jewellery' at the end of the build.

Revell's model represents two different vehicle types… either a 1017 or a 1222. The latter is an all-wheel-drive truck powered by a 220 HP V6 engine. It has an additional transfer case that splits the torque to the axles and has a good front drive axle, which is again a rare feature in a 1/24 or 1/25 kit – adding more appeal, in addition to the crew cab. The 1017 is a more diminutive brother,

TECH SPEC
Mercedes 1222 LF16

Kit: Revell 07655 - Mercedes Benz 1017 LF16
Scale: 1/24
Accessories: CTM 24031 Catwalk type "E", CTM 24049 Wheel chocks, CTM 24190 Marker lights (orange), CTM 24191 Marker lights (red), Fujimi 11505 Garage tools
Notes: Custom made decals drawn by Karel Václavík and printed by Luboš Vinar

again a 4x4 truck but with a smaller 170 HP six-cylinder engine. However, the kit deals with the engine only by using a different transfer of the door badges (1017 or 1222). There is just one engine supplied and that is the smaller in-line six. My choice was driven by the colour I wanted to use on it, and that was fluorescent orange. Not all vehicles wore this shade but the Austrian 1222 from the city of Hard did, so I had new decals made. These were drawn by my friend Karel Václavík and printed by Luboš Vinar. They both did a great job and I had the decals in the post in the matter of days, and it was a real pleasure to work with them.

14.2 QUICK CHASSIS WORK

As the whole chassis is covered with the cab and body, I did not spend any extra time with building and detailing it apart from some basic witness mark cleaning and sanding, so didn't bother with any attempts at making a V6 engine for the 220 version. On the bumper, which is properly visible, I did not like that the headlamps were just shallow, so I cut through the aperture and added small boxes where the light parabolas would be. Once painted with Molotow Liquid Chrome these displayed more realistic depth. Clear parts were used without any modification.

14.3 CAB

The cab and interior construction were simple too; cab shell is one piece so there is no need for any filling and sanding. The cab exterior got new wipers, which were slightly modified original plastic arms and photo-etched wi-

1. The vehicle chassis was built as per the instructions.

2. One of the very few kit modifications was to open the slots in the grille.

3. If you are not super enthusiastic about fire engines the interior is detailed enough.

5-6. The fire extinguisher comes from the Italeri accessories set, and the phone was supplied in the kit. Only the cord was added.

4. Although 30 years old, the one-piece cab shell was beautifully detailed. All it needed before painting was a primer.

1. Although spartan, with some careful painting of the details made the interior authentic enough.

2. A dark green wash was used to highlight the ribbed seat structure.

3. Pigments were applied on the floor, indicatimg that the vehicle may not necessarily be operated in a clean environment.

4. Despite the kit's age the painted interior still looks the part.

5. Mr.Color 173 Fluorescent orange was the right colour for the job.

6. As the original kit decals were old and cracked, new ones were drawn and printed.

pers from a classic KFS set. On the grille, all the apertures were opened by removing the material from the back using a Proxxon hand grinder, followed by fine sanding. The large working light on the A pillar was detailed with a bulb fashioned from a piece of clear sprue. The background was painted with Molotow Liquid Chrome. As for the interior, the kit has all it needs. I just added tread plate on the floor and the stowage box between the front seats. The telephone is straight from the kit, and just

the curved cable was added, while the fire extinguisher comes from Italeri Accessories set No.720. The original kit does not contain any decals for gauges as the details are moulded straight onto the dashboard panel, so there was space for traditional hand painting via a fine brush and Vallejo acrylics. Signal lights and buttons on the dash were picked out with the brush too, but the strip of signal lights along the upper edge of the dash was cut to size from an old Italeri F12 Volvo dash decal.

The rest of the decals inside the cab consisted of KFS data plates and spare KFS/Italeri logos. The interior was treated with a dust wash on the floor and lower areas, grey filter over the dashboard, and dark brown filters and wash applied over the seats, while pigments were added on the floor. The kit windshield suffered from deep fractures that were easy to see and impossible to remove, so I had to make my own one from a piece of clear sheet. The rest of the kit clear parts were OK.

14.4 BODY CONSTRUCTION

Body construction is pretty simple – basically just four walls, floor and roof. The rear has all the details including the lights moulded and the only parts that needed work were the ladders (including their racks) and the railing. The floor holds a pair of mudguards, taillights and reflectors, and water pump outlets. All was left straight from the box except for the roof diamond plate structure, which was simply too rough in comparison to what PE parts would allow. This needed the railing mounts to be made new, as the old item was sanded away when removing the diamonds from the roof – and the ladder racks mount to be cut away and added over the bent photo-etched sheet applied over the rack sides. It all was a little tricky and took two evenings' work, but the fineness of the PE tread plate covering the whole body was worth it.

The side steps, again, feature tread plate structure, so the plastic was replaced with folded PE sheet. I used 1mm plastic sheet and scratch-built the basic part rather than removing all the moulded detail on the original kit parts. I also made some of the lockers and hose mounts from the same CTM PE tread plate and added a CTM PE wheel chock as well. The hose came straight from the kit and looked surprisingly good for its age. Retaining

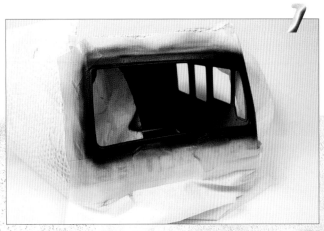

1. Flat black was used on the carefully masked windscreen rubber.

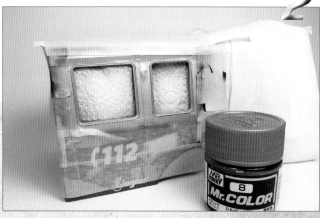

2. The side window frames provided a nice enhancement in silver.

3. The last step was to seal the decals with a coat of gloss varnish.

4. Once all the parts had been painted the assembly was simple and straightforward.

5. Wipers often need to be replaced in older kits.

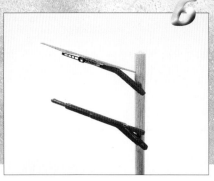

6. For easier installation I sometimes keep the original plastic arm and only use the etched blade.

7. The fine details of the PE parts cannot be matched by anything in plastic.

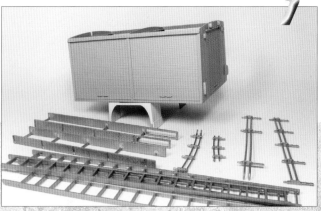

1. Detailed enough, the body exterior was built straight from the box.

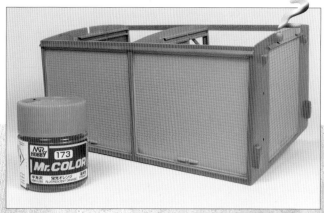

2. Spraying the orange was the first step of the body painting.

3. Then all the orange was masked and the exterior silver parts were sprayed.

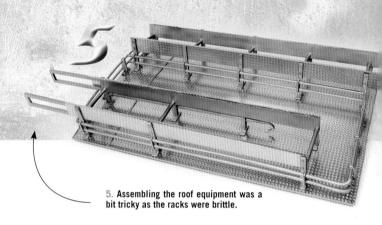

5. Assembling the roof equipment was a bit tricky as the racks were brittle.

6. Replacing the treadplate pattern with PE sheets was repeated on the side steps but the hose came straight from the kit.

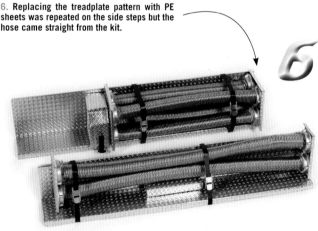

4. Moulded treadplate on the roof was replaced with etched CTM plates. The ladder rack mounts were scratch-built.

straps were made from black electric tape and etched buckles from CTM 24046 set for curtainsider trailers.

The right-hand side of the body comes with the shutter door separate and allows the possibility of leaving them open – and provides a basic interior and equipment. My plan was to leave it either closed or open and build a part of the interior from scratch, depending on how the project progressed, so I left this until the very end right before attaching the

roof to the body and the body to the chassis. I was enjoying the build a lot, so I thought it was worth spending several more evenings on detailing the body interior. I had reference photos available showing that the rear part of the body contains the pump and all the plumbing, which is quite specific, and it does not give a modeller much freedom. The front part of the body, on the other hand, contains usually just shelves and racks where all sorts of equipment is stored, and this can differ from

one vehicle to another. Therefore, I employed the usual modeller's licence here rather than following anything real, and just used what I had available and what I thought would look appropriate. Most of the original kit parts from the interior cannot be used efficiently, as they are usually just a relief on the surface.

I made all the interior walls and shelves from CTM PE tread plate. The rack with drawers were made of plastic and detailed with photo-etched tread plate and KFS hand-

TECH-TIP: REALISTIC LIGHTS

Lights are a very important part of each model. The elementary principle common to most kits is that there is a basic plastic component over which a clear plastic lens is applied. In that case it is up to the modeller to paint the light background authentically. A common method is using plain silver paint, but bare metal foil or any properly chromed paint looks much more realistic. Often there is a chance to add a bulb made of a piece of clear sprue to increase the detail level. The following photos provide will hopefully provide inspiration on how lights can be detailed or enhanced.

1 Adding depth to the headlights means an additional box needs to be built inside the bumper.

2 The mirror surface on the lights was painted with Molotow Liquid chrome.

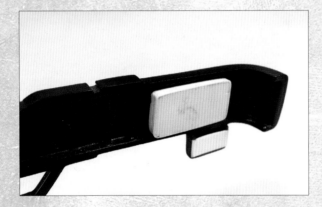

3 Bulbs can be added into the deeper lights and are a viable enhancement.

4 Tamiya clear blue is a good choice for beacons and emergency lights on emergency vehicles.

DONE!

The chromed surface adds depth and realism to the clear lamps. Note the bulb is clearly visible on the model.

5 Clear paints are suitable for tail lamps, indicator lights and such.

6 CTM etched lamps come with polyurethane lenses and do not need any preparation before application.

AND HERE ARE A COUPLE OF OTHER EXAMPLES!

1 Bare metal foil is a quick and easy way to make realistic light backgrounds.

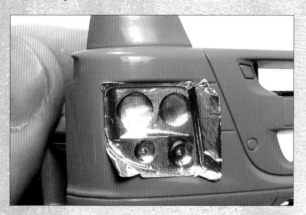

2 Combining it with PE lamps is simple and effective.

3 Milling all sorts of marker lights in a Proxxon mill can be very effective, especially when it comes to American classics or European custom trucks.

4 In this lamp the BM foil was used as a background, and the bulb was made from a piece of clear sprue.

les, and the large toolbox comes from the Garage & Tools set made by Fujimi. Jerry cans were sourced from the old 1/24 Tasca set and the large yellow cans were from the original kit and just simply modified. The large plastic box on the upper shelf is a 3D-printed item, and was given to me by Adam Berkes. The boots I got were cast in resin, but I believe these were originally available in an unidentified kit, while warning triangles were from the painted CTM 24118 kit.

There are all sorts of lights all around the model, beacons, marker lights and so on. For the headlamps, Molotow Liquid Chrome was used; beacons come in clear plastic so just a clear blue from Mr.Color was applied in few layers, while the taillights were just moulded as part of the rear body wall. On these, silver paint was applied first over which Tamiya transparent red and orange paints were added. In addition, PE CTM lights were used all

1. The ladders were painted with Mr.Color 119 Sand yellow, followed with a hair spray.

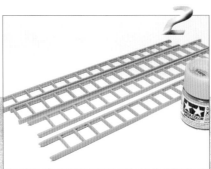

2. Flat acrylic yellow was used as a top coat.

3. Once dry, the ladders were chipped to show the wooden surface underneath the paint.

4. One of the side panels was left open to show the interior walls, built from etched CTM treadplate.

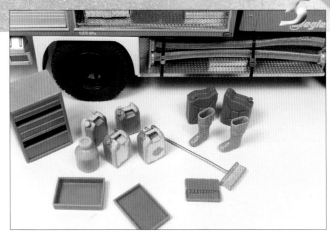

5. Accessories were taken from the spares box, and are in fact not specifically firefighting equipment, but it still looks good and authentic.

around the model. Additional taillights under the body come from CTM set 24135 and the reflectors are from CTM 24098. Marker lights all around the vehicle were provided by CTM 24190.

14.5 ORANGE FLAVOUR

Painting the model was as straightforward as building it. I didn't want to any experiment in any way, so I kept everything strictly within the limits of familiarity. All the paints were either Mr.Color or Tamiya, diluted with Mr.Color Leveling thinner. The only exception was the ladders, which were chipped using the hairspray technique; the yellow topcoat was therefore diluted with Tamiya acrylic thinner. All black on the model is via Mr.Surfacer Finishing Black, which is great as a primer but works well enough as a regular matt black too. What really makes this model is the specific fluorescent orange – Mr.Color 173 Fluorescent Orange. It comes as semi-gloss and once the decals were applied it was sealed with gloss clear Dupli Color varnish, which comes in a spray can, but I decanted it and then airbrushed it to ensure more control. Sealing the decals demanded layering and sanding between the individual varnish layers, and the final coat was afforded extra lustre by using Tamiya polishing compounds. There was much masking involved in painting this model. All the windows have either rubber seals or an aluminium frame, which needed patience… the curved corners especially. What made it easier, on the other hand – and saved time – was the amount of PE tread plate used all around and it was nickel plated, therefore it didn't need any painting. What emerged as a great solution for accentuating small details accurately was Molotow Liquid Chrome, which was used when hand painting the star logo on the grille. Once the vehicle was assembled, black oil paint wash highlighted the cab panel lines.

The oil paint use for weathering on this model was truly minimalistic. Fire engines are always kept clean, dry and safe so any weathering can only take place when vehicles get dirty in action. An oil paint wash was used to highlight the side wall lettering and the tread, and some deposits were painted on the tyre edges, representing mud and general dirt. The lower edges of the mudguards and mud flaps were weathered using good old speckling, and the exhaust rust (which is barely visible on the finished model) was executed with a Lifecolor set.

CONCLUSION

All in all, building this model would have been almost out-of-the-box if it hadn't been for the overly rough treadplate on the plastic parts. Fire engines in general are a rather specific genre of models that may not be for everyone. However, I have discovered their magic and detailing potential. Revell's kit, despite its vintage, can easily be built into a good-looking model without any need for complex conversions and loads of accessories. ▪

15 MODEL GALLERY

Jiri Hübner	Ford AA Wrecker
Jiri Hübner	AEC Matador
Ladislav Petrik	Renault R340
Ladislav Petrik	Volvo F89
Jiri Hübner	Mack AC Crane
Jiri Hübner	White Frightliner
Jiri Hübner	Mack AC

By: Jiri Hübner

Tech Spec
Ford AA Wrecker

Kit: Ford AA, limited resin kit from Jiri Hübner and Jan Mostek
Scale: 1/25
Notes: Scratch-built wrecker body, cab converted to soft top, decals drawn by Jan Mostek

By: Jiri Hübner

SPEC
AEC Matador

Kit: KFS AEC Matador
Scale: 1/24
Notes: Scratch-built logging crane body, decals drawn by Jan Mostek

By: Ladislav Petrik

TECH SPEC
Renault R340

Kit: Italeri Renault 771, Italeri Cargo trailer 3885
Scale: 1/24
Notes: Scratch-built six-cylinder engine, trailer coupling system and rear air suspension, trailer wheels from Revell racing trailer, trailer air suspension from Italeri Cargo trailer, Heller axles

By: Ladislav Petrik

TECH SPEC
Volvo F89

Kit: KFS Volvo F89
Scale: 1/24
Notes: Frame front end based on Italeri Volvo F12, modified Italeri engine, scratch-built rear suspension,
KFS split rims on Volvo, real balsa wood load, scratch-built trailer

By: Jiri Hübner

TECH SPEC
Mack AC Crane

Kit: Monogram Mack AC
Scale: 1/25
Notes: Extended wheelbase, scratch-built crane body manufactured by The Universal Crane Company, Cleveland, Ohio. Decals drawn by Jan Mostek.

By: Jiri Hübner

TECH SPEC
White Freightliner

Kit: AMT White Freightliner SD, AMT Double header trailers
Scale: 1/25
Notes: CTM 005 White Freightliner details set, KFS resin wheels, converted into version with radiator placed behind the cab, real aluminium trailer side walls, decal drawn by Jan Mostek

By: Jiri Hübner

Mack AC

Kit: Monogram Mack AC
Scale: 1/25
Notes: cab reworked to early version, custom made photo etched parts, scratch-built wheels, vehicle built per reference photos from telescope mirror transport for Mount Wilson observatory in California in 1917